Noah

FIRST TIME BOATER ARkER – PHILOSOPHER A not what you think book!

VIGGO P. HANSEN

authorHOUSE®

AuthorHouse™
1663 Liberty Drive
Bloomington, IN 47403
www.authorhouse.com
Phone: 1-800-839-8640

First published by AuthorHouse 1/15/2010

ISBN: 978-1-4490-6642-0 (e)
ISBN: 978-1-4490-6643-7 (sc)
ISBN: 978-1-4490-6639-0 (hc)

Library of Congress Control Number: 2009914340

Printed in the United States of America
Bloomington, Indiana

This book is printed on acid-free paper.

Published by
Dreams and Hopes
1119 Akron Street
San Diego, CA 92106

ACKNOWLEDGEMENT

Even though this Noah saga was divinely inspired, it did not always come with proper grammar and syntax. So help was needed – here are the folks that generously provided derisive remarks and fine tuning: Alex, Anne, Carol, Debora, Dixie, Edith, Erich, John, Kimo, Leesa and Mark. There was a host of others who did not want their reputation sullied by association, I respect their wishes. So to you all, you are hereby recognized and thanked – your help was indeed scholarly and invaluable.

Viggo Pete Hansen

CONTENTS

REVELATION AND DEDICATION

Every sailor and wanna-be sailor, whether they know it or not, is in direct contact with a personal god or gods - however many there may be. What we sailors fail to appreciate is that the gods are constantly trying to get in touch with us, but we ignore their messages since we are either too busy sailing or drinking beer. Keep this thought firmly in mind next time you untie your dock lines.

Indeed it was a dark and eerie night when I was directly contacted (after a nip or two) by some god and directed to tell the entire world what really happened to our erstwhile arker-sailor hero - buddy Noah. This is for sure a shocking revelation that has given new meaning to my day sailing life in the San Diego harbor. I was divinely pressured, with many or else's, to pass this poignant revelation on to the global boating community. Truly it is a most incredible sailing saga whose intent was simply to bring clarity of life's purpose to all who venture on the waters – fresh, salty, still or turbulent – and with cosmic implications.

If you believe in a linear flow of time, then every event may have a beginning; e.g. to go sailing you begin by casting off your lines - duh. What every sailing spirit seeks is any reason whatsoever to go sailing, seldom do we ask why and how it began or what it portends for the future. We see it as fun – but for dear old Noah it was not hilarious.

So why do we go sailing, is it to get away from daily woes, beat the bejeesus out of someone else's boat and crew - or is it perhaps an inborn desire to commune with the cosmos? Most sailors I know tend to be deeply philosophical, especially with libation.

Perhaps the answer to this ageless enigma, of why we sail, can be found in an astonishing event many have forgotten, i.e. Noah's cruise as the world's first time arker/boater. Indeed boating took on real meaning during a massive drowning event, initiated by a deeply ticked off God and his dear lovely Goddess. They wisely chose Noah, then an unknown man of the desert – to become history's first time boater.

Having forgotten most of King Jim's Noah biography it was time to revisit the great book Genesis, study original manuscripts, interview scholars, pursue the latest research and then generously share findings with today's sailors. I quickly discovered that creation details depended on whose version of the earth's beginnings you are comfortable with; however, the results are equally confusing.

It was reassuring to discover a general consensus among multiple versions of Genesis that Noah was in fact a bona fide novice boater. Since the details are totally lacking, I also found absolutely no evidence of anyone having properly acknowledged Noah for his many courageous seafaring feats as well as his philosophical insights and deeply personal conversations with God. Only through spiritual enlightenment did I become energized and dedicated to tell you Noah's story.

Noah was not only a sailor's sailor, or more correctly an arker's arker, he was an insightful metaphysics philosopher who dabbled and wrestled with heady life and death issues, primarily as related to multiple drownings in a desert. Noah's personal concern, from his early childhood in the dunes had to do with what really is, "The Big Picture." When Noah met God in his humble desert tent, he knew beyond doubt that he was in touch with somebody who could help him understand the meaning of life and the purpose of the universe, including sailing. This became a "wow" moment for arker Noah.

Stunned and overwhelmed by the information revealed to me that dark and eerie night, it was time to go to work. Since there are few credible sources I was free to embellish my revelation of Noah's epic arking episode. And so it is most appropriate that this reconstruction of Noah's adventure be dedicated to him and his beloved wife Sarah, who after some forty days of incessant showers began bobbing aimlessly about, on a water soaked desert, in a leaky homemade ark while unselfishly saving pairs of God's creatures from drowning. Oh the logistics.

Everyone who goes to sea, whether they get sick (most do) or not, will be inspired by Noah's straight-on, no nonsense approach to ark building, navigation, billeting, entertaining and counseling a menagerie greater in numbers than today's San Diego Zoo - and all the while sailing blithely to nowhere. Actually, this description does sound much like any afternoon cruise in today's local bay, river, lake or pond.

In his time, Noah was considered a gutsy naval architect and seafarer. However, today's sailors lazily - buy - instead of constructing as Noah did - a big expensive yacht that we can only afford at the expense of our kid's dental work. We may not know how to sail it, but we gleefully load it to the gunnels with cheap beer and chips. Finally we populate our precious heavily mortgaged boat with dimwitted buddies mislabeled as crew and promptly, like Noah, sail off to nowhere.

This unabridged reconstructed saga, based on personal revelation, focuses on; 1) God Almighty and his universe, 2) his strikingly knockout gorgeous Goddess, 3) Arker Noah, 4) his intensely logical wife Sarah, 5) a devilish clever egocentric peregrine, known as Falc, and 6) an irreverent happy-go-lucky hummingbird, aptly dubbed Hummy. Their collective experiences aboard a homemade leaky ark, filled with pairs of God's chosen critters to survive a massive shower have forever redefined what it means to be a sailor, tar, gob, mariner, seaman, swab, arker, crewmember, philosopher and professional liar.

With no humility whatsoever, I hereby dedicate this godly inspired revelation to: Captain Noah - the man who was fully in charge of an ark while most of the world drowned. The inspired message here is to simply insure that Noah's nautical contributions and philosophical insights are not lost in sand dunes and will forever serve as an inspiration to all aspiring and intrepid (i.e. scared) sailors. To all boaters/arkers – let Captain Noah be your nautical and spiritual guide.

Skoal, Ciao, Salute, bottoms up to ---to you --- Captain Noah

Before we embark –

Please dear readers understand that in order for me to properly share this magnificent revelation with you many minor liberties were granted me, both in modern and oldie English usage and facts. Noah's story flips between a long time ago and today. Actually there are many similarities as you will see. Furthermore my godly revelations were often fuzzy in details.

CHAPTER 1

THE BEGINNING

My revelation begins with a historical perspective and is mostly told in the present tense. It is true that the clear irresistible clarion call attracting hordes of humans into boating is rooted in the fact that life began, after the Big Ka-Boom, in a liquid environment, i.e. the oceans. Even today, following the usual and preferred conception methods, techniques and slipups - animals begin life sloshing around in a nice tepid salt-water solution called the amniotic fluid until it is time to independently begin breathing polluted air without a hose attached to a female.

However, our primordial wet experience, though difficult for most to remember, is never completely erased from our long term memory cells. Since this is true, it is only natural that we continue to "yearn to return" to those halcyon carefree moments of thrashing about in a warm saline elixir, nourished with flavored sweet mother's milk. Today many sailors equate this earlier experience to an adult cruise with Club Med.

Ah-so - we are all born wanna-a-be sailors because of these early in vitro comfy experiences. However, shortly after our birth, and due to capricious mixing of genetic materials, along with governmental educational practices that leaves everyone behind, most humans quickly stray wildly from the Maker's idyllic Garden of Eden concept. After Adam & Eve figured out what was under their fig leaf, a population explosion occurred naturally. Then, wouldn't you know it, people straightaway began beating the daylights out of each other, clearly exemplified by the dysfunctional brothers Cain and Abel's sibling tiffs, that finally led then to a really nasty climax.

Needless to say, this aberrant and ungrateful human behavior was anathema to the beneficent Creator's grandiose plan of blessed harmony, replete with hissing asps, organic clothing and restrictions on apple munching. But once these naive primitive folks began dropping their leafy drawers, listening to conniving snakes, and got into eating applesauce, mankind's maudlin history quickly followed. Sex, apples and snakes sold then and still do today. Today the difference is - many snakes have law degrees.

Perhaps about 5,000 or so years ago, as believed by some King Jimers, God and Goddess Almighty became clinically despondent with the incessant political and religious bickering among all their now mostly nude creatures. However it was primarily the carnivores, dominated by know it all humans who rebelliously evolved way beyond the Garden of Eden's ban on eating sweet red Macintosh apples. Instead they greedily evolved to eating raw, juicy red meat, later to become medium rare. Not only that, but they also began listening and taking advice from hissing asps, who evolved to become renowned bankers, legal counselors and financial advisors.

These rebellious and downright ungodly activities, highlighted by one spirited religious war after another; each war designed and ballyhooed to end all wars, led to a celestial crisis. "Enough already", said the generous Creator Almighty God. He decreed that a momentous meteorological event was to occur, as clearly chronicled in Genesis OT. OT is Old Testament (not overtime) for you sports fans.

You surely cannot blame a benevolent God for becoming testy. An aside, it was also revealed to me that it was not the apple's fault that sex and wars became glorified sporting events. Apples have finally been exonerated and evolved to become a significant health food based on their rich natural organic ingredients, but only after overcoming a controversial biblical history. As we today know, apple strudel and apple cider are accepted as nutritional and tasty, but it wasn't always so. Sorry for the digression. God's more profound problems centered on life and death issues and apples were but an irritant along with serpents and scratchy loose fitting green apparel.

Ungrateful, narcissistic, and bad mannered animals thought God; where did the missus and I go so wrong? This searing morality question became an obsession with God. He felt ethically obligated to do something, even if it was wrong. What the hey, thought God, I have already made one major creation snafu, irreverently referred to as my Big Ka-Boom; so whatever I do now, surely cannot be much worse.

"You know Goddess; I really must have made some egregious miscalculations in our erstwhile glorious creation scheme that has allowed animals to stray in so many off-the-chart directions. Was it the mischievous DNA molecule - that funky double helix thing that betrayed me? I for sure never anticipated probabilities that seemingly allow for so many strange permutations. You know, there really is no end to probabilities, is there?"

"My dear God Almighty, do not be so hard on yourself for this unholy mess. The almost infinite probabilities lurking in your tricky molecules are truly difficult to comprehend. Let me gently remind you Dear, since you flunked developmental math three times, perhaps if you had tried a fourth time you might have passed and saved yourself this heart rendind grief. Flunking math is like shooting oneself in the foot, eh Big Guy?"

"You are so right my precious Goddess, I really did OK in single digit addition and subtraction, it was multiplication and division that were my mathematical Achilles heel. What shall we now do about this immorality soup we are in?" Asks a deeply troubled God, meekly seeking solace from his ever trusting, gorgeous, faithful and understanding Goddess. She was so smart – and cute.

God, having been an early-on feminist by creating the first women from man's ribs, pleaded with his Goddess to partner in some serious discussions on the evolutionary debacle occurring since their creation. But they agreed to omit any reference to mathematical stuff. They further agreed that humans were now totally consumed by slaying, slewing and begetting - and this unsavory process was accelerating. Begetting had become essential to sustain the escalating slew and slay business. Was the problem really a faulty DNA, a topic God was not going to discuss since it might also reflect on a defect in male ribs? This line of inquiry could backfire. They indeed had a tangled problem, but assigning fault was something the Two did not want to explore.

The ever gentle sweet Goddess suggested they first try adding some romantic activities, like drawing, music, line and square dancing to help civilize their earthly miscreants. God thought this was a powerful idea and so they began to surreptitiously educate humans in the "fine arts." Initially, these primitive art forms consisted of colorful cave paintings and rhythmically beating together small flat river rocks. This rock music was challenging since it often resulted in sore thumbs.

Art really did catch on, but not as they had hoped. The God and Goddess's arty ideas quickly led to salacious literature (dirty stories), bongo music (rap) and nude art (porn). Sadly these well meaning artistic efforts spurred the mucho-macho slayers and slewers to new heights of mayhem, now emboldened by primitive Souza drum beats and naughty cave finger paintings. Wars were exciting and glorified heroic killing events creating pitiful literature, garish music and gawd awful gruesome murals. Museums proliferated to house this "artsy" stuff. Wars became accepted as the preferred method of maintaining social order. Much of this slaughtering was done in the name of a variety of emerging gods who constantly agreed to disagree. The original God and Goddess rightfully concluded, "How wacky is this?"

Dung (not dang) became God's favorite and personally guarded expression as he daily surveyed his run amok creations eagerly procreating in order to quickly kill each other. This steamy and stormy repetitive cycle of sex and violence was clearly ungodly and personally embarrassing for a peace loving God and Goddess. Furthermore all this warring activity naturally led to extravagant over consumption depleting precious natural resources. The entire earth was in physical jeopardy and moral decay. It had to be stopped – but how?

By golly, agreed the God and Goddess, if art doesn't work let us as a last ditch desperate effort try scaring the willies out of these misfits by introducing the un-comfortable features of going to hell - if they don't repent and improve. Results of these scare tactics were totally ineffective, eating fatty foods even increased, wars and sex continued unabated. Bad jokes prevailed. "I am going to hell to play golf and beat the brains out of my buddies."

Philistines (the stock brokers of that day) thrived by brokering bets on the reality of hell – safe bets since it was an unknown, until you died. However, if you were uneasy about a potential hellish future you could invest in "Get the Hell out of Hell" futures cards. These became an economic bonanza with no refunds. And so the big top three ring circuses rolled on, clowns, lawyers, quacks, freaks and politicians alike plied their chicanery, all taking advice from snake oil soothsayers in the name of their god. Vipers to this day still get a bum rap since they always seem involved with issues of morality.

Time passed ever so painfully and slowly for the chagrined, distraught, and guilt ridden God and Goddess. Then one brilliant starlit night, when God, in a restless but reflective mood while sipping His cognac, decided to again discuss this irksome situation with His beautiful long haired emerald eyed understanding Goddess. After all, it was her that had conjured up fine arts, which hadn't worked any better than His concept of eternal damnation. Each had tried their heavenly best to instill civility in their creations without much success.

God had delayed this verbal confrontation for fear His Goddess would blame Him for the entire mess, since He had indeed created the universe, the Goddess and humans, while simultaneously flunking basic math. A perfect celestial storm. The Goddess who was demurely waiting in the wings - so to speak - was also eager to address this nagging moral problem, but certainly wanted to stay clear of any sensitive rib talk, as well as God's occasional uncontrolled wrath.

This time God charged straightaway into the nettlesome topic by suggesting it was high time to begin a major earthly rehab to correct the ungodly activities now festering in their beautiful Garden of Eden. "We have gone from art to hell, neither worked, it is now time for one gosh darn awful rainstorm, followed by a humongous flood and really begin creation anew." Proclaims the frustrated and suddenly re-energized God Almighty. Cognac can do that. "This will be a new Genesis, Beta Version Number 2. And this time I will micro manage it and you Goddess will leave snide math asides the hell out of it!"

"Oh dear God, oops, sorry God, l didn't mean to take your name in vain." Blurted the startled Goddess, as she choked on her half-full glass of merlot. She had taken to drinking vintage wine since Post Eden there remained some lingering uncertainty about fermented apple juice's long term affects on one's sense of decency and intellectual curiosity. God and Goddess had agreed that at least for now wine was fine and indeed it became her drink of choice at their private heavenly happy hour.

The Goddess reluctantly agrees that all this unseemly mayhem is bordering on chaos and must cease, but she was not at all comfortable with God's impetuously proposed "rainy season" deconstructionists approach. Although Goddess is not an engineer and also never succeeded at remedial math, she intuitively senses many hydraulic problems associated with all that water sloshing around in their high desert, but doesn't want to go there with God's current rambunctious mood. But something has to be done, and done soon. After lengthy and intense discussions, she concurs with God's master plan. "I'll dig out our galoshes and slickers in the morning; now let us get some rest. By the way I do have a splitting headache tonight." Dung.

Next morning the God and Goddess together prepare a first draft designed to swiftly undo what had happened to their original bucolic Garden of Eden. The Goddess sadly reminisced about her once luscious arboretum that had yielded sweet red Macintosh apples, shiny green fig leaf butt covers and provided a homey habitat for all those cute slinky hissing spitting vipers. We must begin anew they optimistically agree, while savoring their breakfast of Godly fortified oatmeal and enriched lo-fat camel yogurt.

"You bet, my dear Goddess, it is out with the old and in with the new and while we are at it we will keep pesky mathematics out of the new world, no more pi-s, unless they are apple, ha ha – a little funny to begin the new day." chortles the charged up God.

"Let me again warn you about maligning mathematics." Warns the Goddess. "Take pride Dear, you did really well with your finger and toe counting. Always remember that mathematics is made by and for the Gods, and you are truly doing OK, you just need to do your homework more often."

"Thanks Kid. I needed that reassurance on this glorious morning." says God. The God and Goddess's renovation scheme required many more creative measures than simply drowning ungrateful and misbehaving earthly bums. "First, I must find an inside leader." muses God. "Otherwise, if these human rascals get a hint of the proposed liquid calamity headed their way, they may all start building arks and bobbing around and I will never catch them, we would be faced with a massive ark "sail away ha ha" problem. No, I must select a leader quickly and secretly get our project under way. Initially I will choose and test this desert nomad guy, Noah. I have been watching him for some time; he is sort of smart, but not too smart and I think he is deathly scared of water. These are the qualities of a good ark captain."

God's draft plan evolved quite simply, drown everybody; except for this one poor ne'er-do-well camel driver named Noah, his sharp-tongued wife Sarah, a few of their lazy kids, and one female and one male of every species. Then start anew by having these selected pairs engage in making whoopee. But what are the probabilities that this will work any better than before, wonders a somewhat skeptical math phobic God. Just what are the chances? Stop it – I must leave math out of this.

The drowning schema was to become a monumental water works project, eclipsing the Chinese Three Gorges dam of later times.

God mentally envisioned Noah constructing the world's biggest ark ever, and loading it up with lucky designated survivor pairs. Then it would rain and rain for some forty days and nights creating a massive body of water that would float the ark. The plan was perfect, or so it seemed at the time.

Reflections: Today every single, married and/or otherwise sexually connected, sailor owes Noah their gratitude. It was this naive humble man of the big dusty desert, who was handpicked by the God and Goddess to save just one couple of every meat eating and vegan species from extinction through excessive water consumption.

Noah's resume clearly revealed he had no prior naval education or experience in ways of deep blue waters, although, like cats, he innately knew to stay on top of the murky water at the oasis where he regularly tanked his camels. He also knew by instinct that anytime you get into water deeper than your midriff, you must react fast.

It is believed that aversion to sinking in water is a genetically hard wired trait found in everyone who puts to sea, regardless of the size of his or her boat – or brain. As the adage goes, do not let the water in your boat get above your belly button. It was Noah's obsessive "fear of water" that raised him to number one standing in God's search and screen process to find an ark captain for the coming deluge.

As we now go on to extensively explore nomad Noah's exciting nautical life, it is my fervent wish that we remember and honor this ark-man of the sea, who was exclusively selected by God because he was hydrophobic and God was set on drowning everyone. Perfect match - survival depends on not drowning. Noah would go on to boldly demonstrate that there is hope for everyone to become a proficient ark sailor, even first time out, as long as they remain petrified of drowning.

Noah proved the ultimate nautical truism.

"Folks with drowning phobias make better sailors."

We Begin.

CHAPTER 2

THE BIG ANNOUNCEMENT

A rugged bearded sand dune landlubber of long ago, by the simple name of Noah, arose sleepily one sun drenched morning in his godforsaken tattered windblown tent, loosely tethered on one of the arid knolls in the unknown Rat-a-tat Desert. Like a newly aroused cat, Noah rubbed tear moistened sand from his eyes with clenched fists. Oh, boy thought the ever optimistic Noah - another jolly day in our windy dusty desert begins anew. "I just can't wait to go a-romping in the dunes."

Noah's wife Sarah, no beauty queen at this time of day, arose more slowly and got the coffee pot boiling without muttering a word. As though she had a premonition of what was to happen she did not exude Noah's jolliness. Quite the contrary. Sarah remained dour while the coffee pot gurgled nosily away filling their homey little tent with its familiar refreshing aroma. Nothing like fresh coffee in the morning.

Soon the squatting Noah was leisurely smoking his stinky old hookah and enjoying his wife's first cup of freshly brewed coffee. Life in the early morning desert was a good time for Noah. Sarah was busily shuffling around in a typical pale grey Bedouin robe still wondering why she was up. But this is pretty much how she felt every morning.

Unnoticed, an imposing, big white bearded Hulk, stealthily enters Noah's tent and from behind taps Noah on his right shoulder. It was a friendly gesture meant to instill camaraderie.

"Aye, what do you want?" Noah grumbles rather abruptly as he did not like to be bothered while drinking his first morning coffee and simultaneously inhaling deeply on rancid tobacco fumes. It had been a dark and windy night with fine grained sand oozing in everywhere. The camels had been unusually restless and tried repeatedly to get into Noah and Sarah's small tent. Shooing away stinky camels while trying to sleep leads to crankiness in the morning. Noah needed his space.

"Hey there Noah, ole buddy, do you know who I am?" Came a spirited greeting from the intruding - Big Guy - who presented a majestic figure in Noah's diminutive tent.

Noah, now agitated at this early morning "guess who I am" game and knowing there were few nomads roaming about in the dunes at this time of day, turns around in disgust and is startled to see this glowing white haired apparition facing him and lets out a loud banshee howl, "Oh my god, if it isn't God!"

Noah's, up to this moment drowsy and speechless wife Sarah, had not seen the large intruder, but being a devoted believer in theocracy, screams back at Noah; "Watch your irreverent language or God will getch-ya, you insufferable heathen desert rat."

"What do you mean Sarah, this guy in our charming cozy tent sure looks like God Almighty himself, so listen up?" Replies Noah in a resounding but trembling voice.

"You are losing it Noah, drink your coffee, smoke your foul hookah and think good clean healthy thoughts, eh?" Responds the sleepy, but supremely logical, Noah's ever-loving Sarah. Her night had not been all that swift. She had actually been the one up chasing away bad breath camels that wanted in their tent. Camels are by nature loving animals that would often shower Sarah with camel affection by slobbering her face. Today Sarah was butt tired and not up to any godly attendance issues.

"Shish" snorts Noah.

God, holding out his hands in good will gesture, suddenly finds that his intrusion has stuck Him in the middle of a rapidly escalating spousal snit and deftly attempts to calm the rising storm. "Hold it gang, we have a magnificent day full of opportunities looming before us, but we also have a major problem facing us and so we need to be united. I am truly sorry I did not let you know beforehand that I was coming to visit you on this beautiful warm dewy morning. The dunes seem to be full of "get up and go" music."

All is momentarily quiet as Sarah has turned around and faces God, eye ball to eye ball. She becomes understandably flabbergasted, speechless, her jaw drops and she faints dead away, muttering, "Good God Almighty, now what?"

"What the h….?" Noah was going to risk using the "h" word, but luckily for him, he at the last second thought better of it. Noah's immediate thoughts and language skills began to deteriorate over the simultaneous appearance of God Almighty and his wife's sudden unconsciousness. "My coffee is probably also getting cold. Bad karma for the day"

God is also showing modest discomfort as he hovers over a squatting upset Noah puffing away on his hookah and sees Sarah flat out cold on the brown desert sand. An uneasy feeling tells him that His dire watering message may not be as gleefully received as He had hoped. It had been some time since God had had a one on one conversation with humankind, so He worries that he may have lost his touch. Actually God's last formal contact was when He shooed them out of The Garden for misbehaving. "I must hone my interpersonal skills. Perhaps these folks simply do not understand why I sometimes get My knickers in a knot."

Now in a highly conciliatory voice, God calmly asks Noah, "May I call you Noe? It seems fitting that we get on a more friendly and personal level for our impending discussion. Let me help you get your wife up off the sand and properly prop her against the tent wall. It'll be a lot easier for her to breath in a sitting position - poor thing." A stinking camel sticks his regal head in the tent flap and gives a loud disrespectful snort blowing nasal moisture everywhere. He too, is obviously upset by what has happened to his friend Sarah. Camels have a high regard for women.

Poor Sarah is still totally unconscious and so fails to appreciate God's benevolent magnanimity and His desire to be nice. But after a few moments and without help Sarah slowly recovers, gets up, opens her eyes and again sees God. She lets out an eerie whimper as she for a second time crumples back onto the sand.

God Almighty and Noah look at each other and shrug realizing they can do little at this time for the out of it Sarah, who is again spread eagled. Noah decides to leave her alone.

"Whatever you wish God – is of course OK with me. But this is a terrible way for us to handle my startled and whacked out wife. Sarah is good woman and I'll stand by her." Noah's voice is defiant; nobody has ever caused Sarah to collapse – twice. The camels are grumbling loudly outside Noah's tent. They sense big time trouble.

Sarah remains sprawled out and unconscious while God and Noah shake their heads in resignation. Noah stands erect facing God. "She'll have to sleep it off. But don't You dare try this cockamamie stunt a second time." Warns a stern, but somewhat confused Noah, expressing compassion for wife Sarah while simultaneously showing guarded reverence for God's unannounced early morning intrusion. Noah's coffee is cold.

"Now then God, what is Your big problem that brings You to our humble dust filled tent at this ungodly, oops, godly time of day?" Questions a slowly mellowing but curious Noah, who is now getting a headache, his coffee is cooling, pipe is going out and he feels ashamed about using colorful language in the presence of God. He wonders if Sarah is still completely out of it. Certainly looks that way.

But suddenly Sarah does indeed regain consciousness and explodes at Noah. "What do you mean, this "humble dust filled tent"? I just cleaned it. If you do not like it – next time Buster you can clean it up. I will show you where the gd, oops, sorry God, broom is any time you feel up to using it. You lazy good for nothing males disgust me. Get your own coffee." Sarah rises stiffly, dusts herself off, mats down her hair, rearranges her tattered robe and folds her arms in a typical upset and defiant housewife pose. Look out!

God retreats, realizing how his glorious heavenly life style beats this desert life style. No dust up there. "Oh my dear God, oops, says God, now uneasy and self-conscious about having unconsciously taken his own name in vain. "This is not working out at all." Maybe selecting Noah had been a mistake. God had for sure not wanted to be distracted into a discussion on tent housekeeping chores especially when the mission before Him is to drown everybody.

"What did you say God? Please speak up." Noah is steadily growing restless, impatiently wanting to find out what is God's big conundrum, and why is he, Noah, being stuck with it. However, his state of mind, rattled by Sarah's smart remarks, makes clarity of thought difficult for this simple straight-on man of the desert. Furthermore, he realizes that God and Sarah have the potential of finding a common bond over cleanliness being next to godliness, thus there would be two against him, poor odds when one is God and the other is your wife. "All I said was 'dusty tent', how can that be so cataclysmic?" Groans Noah. "God and his people are becoming just too sensitive."

Finally, Noah decides to take the lead. "OKay, come on God; spit it out, whatever is on Your omniscient mind at this early hour in the morning, we can handle it. Don't let it bother You that You have created a highly volatile and unstable marital situation probably requiring my nearly hysterical wife and me to seek family crises intervention counseling and stress management." God realizes that Noah's statement reeks with sarcasm, but it also hints of Noah's leadership potential. Noah's comments, though somewhat confrontational, are direct and to the point.

"Bottle it Noah, I am definitely not hysterical." Yells the now fully conscious and defiant Sarah. "My tent is the desert's showpiece for homemakers everywhere - having won many awards, including the prestigious Good Tent Keeping."

"Oh, dear," laments God, "I certainly did not intend to disrupt your wonderful down home sand loving folks at this early time of day. I am so sorry, but My heavenly time pieces are notoriously inaccurate. As you don't yet know, but now you will, I and the missus Goddess were the ones responsible for the Big Ka-Boom, or is it Ka-Bang, I always forget. But honestly it has been a downhill run for us ever since. We had such great idyllic dreams and visions that all our precious animals, including you humans, would live in peace and harmony for eternity in our magnificent Garden of Eden. You know, we invested heavily in exotic designer landscapes, including very special fig and apple trees, waterfalls with colorful rocks and chia statues throughout the garden. So homey."

God is drifting and becoming maudlin, yet continues on philosophically. "Let me tell you, We did not anticipate how humans would evolve from our nifty fast acting Ka-Bang event that took place long ago. Exactly when depends on who you listen to, right? And now we can't even agree on when all this started and who really lit the fuse. This has created a God/time warp. The problem is basically mathematical mumbo-jumbo which I do not fully understand beyond single digit finger counting. Life both with and without basic mathematics has become a bummer and now folks keep talking about changing My calendar – the very calendar of My creation events. Do you know how embarrassing and frustrating all this can be; when I don't even know what time it is in My own universe? I really do need help with these problems as well as with all the good for nothing heathens." God rambles.

But continues. "OK, don't get me wrong, a few folks like you and Sarah are super, neat-o, or is it cool, but, my, oh my, most are not. Slewing and slaying has replaced camel racing and falcon hunting as the sports of choice. Can you believe that? The situation is now so untenable and desperate that even the Goddess and I are being forced by egregious moral issues to flood this dusty desert and restart the animal social order all over. However, please appreciate that we do not relish the idea, but it is now a 'must do' assignment. This time the math does add up."

"Whoa there God, ole buddy. What is this I hear? But first, since You nicknamed me Noe - may I call you ole buddy God? Something akin to tit for tat." responds the astonished Noah. Beads of dusty sweat steadily ooze down his dark weather-beaten brow as he tries to understand God's revelation regarding bad behaviors. Noah has survived a tough arid life by being tough. However, he is not comfortable with drowning everybody in his desert just because God and the Goddess have some issues, especially if they resulted from God's poor math skills. "Is it really bad math that causes wars?" wonders Noah. Yes, maybe.

"Sure, sure, Noe, call me Ole Buddy God, we will all need to become really good ole buddies in order to ride out this upcoming rainy season." Smiles the all-wise God, hoping that Noah's cranky demeanor resulted from not finishing his morning coffee and reeking hookah and not from His proposed drowning caper. Noah's snide math comment did not sit well with God either, but perhaps he is right.

So here is the situation in the tent. Noah and Sarah remain speechless while sipping the last bitter dregs of their tepid coffee. Noah's smoldering hookah stinks worse than ever. Sarah, normally gracious, has uncharacteristically failed to offer God a second cup of her coffee. Wafting through the air are the added sounds and unsavory aromas of camels doing their early morning thing outside Noah's tent. Noah and Sarah are afraid of looking each other in the eye for fear they will burst out laughing at the incredulity of God's dilemma along with His proposed solution. It is a tense moment waiting to scream and no one even really knows what time it is.

God is beginning to wonder if Noah and Sarah think this is all some kind of a cosmic joke that will soon blow over with a bunch of belly laughs. "I must get back to serious business."

"So listen up folks, here is the general plan, details **will** follow." asserts God. "As I said, My significant other, the Goddess, and I have decided that We will flood this immense desert with one heck of a shower, lasting forty days and forty nights to be exact. But, before doing so We want you Noah to build an ark of historic proportions and fill it with pairs of frisky animals looking to make whoopee, two by two, as the event promo slogan will clearly state."

"God, this here ark of Yours must surely be a big thing - just what will it look like?" Interrupts the impish Noah, thinking Sarah must have laced the coffee pretty good this morning for him to ask this inane question with a straight face.

"An ark is a big, no huge, vessel Noe, made of strong timbers so that it will float on this ocean that I am going to create right here in the middle of your backyard. The ark will look like a really big upside down elongated wooden tent, some 30 cubits by 150 cubits. I think that is about the size My Missus and I agreed on, but I could be wrong, my number sense tends to be like – you know - inaccurate.

"Ah ha - so tell me more about cubits, God?" asks Noah, while rolling his eyes skyward and looking at Sarah to hopefully brew some hot coffee. "This technical ark-cubit jargon is giving me twinkling twinges between my ears. We need more coffee Sarah."

"Patience Noe, I will explain all that later. But first let me tell you about the spacious ocean in your front yard." Responds God, realizing a cubit has some mathematical implications that He is uncomfortable with. Why did I bring up that detail anyhow?

"Actually Noe My Godly Ocean will probably be more like one big swamp and the only surviving two alligators will be in your boat. Ha, Ha – just a tad of gallows humor to defuse our grim situation. Wait till you hear the rest of the story." Pursues the now again ebullient

God, feeling comfortable that he is finally making progress, but also realizing he is winging it in many places.

"I am not at all certain what this is really about." interjects a quizzical scowling Sarah, while busily sweeping up more drifting sand in her windy tent. Sarah is the type that can knit without a needle. "Guys, let us recap; first, you God, scare me to near death, then my lazy good for nothing husband complains about a dusty tent and finally you suggest flooding the entire desert. Finally You call our soon to be sunk neighborhood a big swamp, and that the only way to survive is to sail merrily away on something dubbed an ark, filled with alligators. Collectively you two males have the brains of a bad omelet. I did not have anything to drink last night, but I sure wish I had – it might help me understand this heavenly madness. Ah, the nobility of drowning."

Sarah momentarily stops to catch her breath and let the sarcasm sink in. "I presume this is just another misguided male solution to a perceived dusty tent problem – you guys crack me up. Let me pour some newly brewed coffee and this time I'll enrich it so we can all thoroughly enjoy going crazy - together. Noah - my beloved twit - why don't you fire up that vile stuff in your hookah? We are all in for an early AM lu-lu session."

"No, no, Sarah, this is a much bigger problem than flooding a dusty tent and making your neighborhood into a desert swamp. Let Me repeat." God is visibly shaken over Sarah's assessment of a deep moral issue. "The Goddess and I are terribly distraught by the manner our creations are treating each other. Seriously, just for kicks, I suggest that you and Noe read the OT and note how many people were killed - by each other – not tigers. Following these idiotic slaughter fests, everyone momentarily stops, lament their fallen pals and wasted bucks; but that moment of remorse soon wears off and then by golly they start the entire nutty process over, all in the name of God – My name.

Go figure. It really upsets me. You know the jingle, an eye for an eye and a tooth for a tooth and the world becomes populated by toothless or root canalled blind folks." God sighs, reaches over and inhales deeply on Noah's hookah. "Good stuff, Noe; and Sarah, your coffee really hits the spot at this tender moment. What did you lace it with? I want my Missus to get some."

"As I was saying this horrendous state of earthly affairs is creating a horde of invalids and poor people too pooped to even enjoy conjugal activities, if you know what I mean? Our idyllic concept of bliss has now become a bottomless ditch populated with lots of dead folks, who died for God's sake. How do you think that makes Me feel, since I am God? If you were eating each other because you were hungry, that we could clearly understand.

Remember, My Goddess and I made everything free in The Garden. Now some of you have concocted business systems to hoard and sell Our free stuff. As a result too many are now impoverished and a few others mega rich. This then led to stabbing and spearing each other so you can all party afterwards on stolen loot. It is beyond belief and – it has to cease. We have painfully witnessed wars beget wars that then became a growth industry necessary for economic growth and stability. You folks never get over one head bashing event till you start another. I and the missus must now assume My God given responsibilities and, by God We will restart the entire operation." God's words are dire and firm but He feels real good about himself. Momentarily he stops pacing, but continues lecturing.

"The decision has been made. This desert is to be flooded, you two and your bratty kids will be the only human survivors; but, and this is a big but, only if Noe here can build a gigantic seaworthy ark. Is that clear?" With a defiant scowl, God shuts up and plops down heavily on the sand floor thinking to Himself, by God I am God. Almost brusquely, "Sarah do you have any more spiked hot coffee?"

"You know God, you are something else. You rightly condemn us lowly humans for amateurishly, but systematically lopping off each other's heads but then your solution is to drown everyone in one big Rat-a-tat desert swimming pool. Cool." Muses Sarah as she gulps down more coffee hoping it will improve her higher order thinking skills enough to clearly understand how massive drowning is more morally acceptable than current slewing and slaying practices. "God, pass me your cup and I'll fill it with my special stuff."

Total silence follows in the tent as Sarah and Noah again look dumb founded as they begin to absorb the full impact of God's pronouncement and what they must now do. Their former sense of frivolity and hilarity is gone, terror is setting in. Noah realizes that his earthy comment on their dusty tent was certainly trivial, out of line and probably upset God, but my Sarah is absolutely right, is God's proposed gully washer really that necessary?

Finally, God breaks the eerie silence with veiled upbeat cheerfulness. "I do have some very exciting news for you two. As I said, you two will be spared drowning by simply building a humongous ark, filling it with pairs of youthful fun loving animals and everyone eagerly looking forward to a full scale action packed cruise right here in your own desert backyard. What could be more thrilling and romantic?"

Sarah is flabbergasted thinking to herself. God has really lost it. We are all doomed.

God continues, "After boarding your beautiful ark, fourty days and thirty-nine nights of incessant rain will follow, which provides an opportune period of time for selfless bonding among your passengers, especially between animals like the mongoose and cobras who often don't understand each other. Then you, Noe, Sarah and your youthful happy-go-lucky menagerie begin cruising on your luxuriously appointed backyard built ark, doing group finger painting, singing Chantilly songs while briskly clapping your hands in gleeful unison. These hilarious participatory 'feel good activities' are guaranteed to keep you and your shipmates from going nuts." God cleverly overlooks the Goddess's artistic failed ventures of earlier times. At times you must overlook past failures or you will become suspect.

"Following a prolonged restful period at sea, the waters will slowly recede back into the desert and you will all joyfully start your lives anew, but without those pesky folks that want to make war and spend money all the time. How is all that for a treat?" God is positively aglow over his incredible plan and begins singing; "A-sailing you will go, ho, ho. A-sailing you will go, ho, ho."

"Yeah, right." responds the fully discombobulated Sarah. "I must have really hit my head hard when I fell a little while ago. As they say, I should be much better when the swelling goes down and Your torrential refreshing rains commence.

While Sarah remains bewildered, Noah is ebullient and has sucked all the smoke out of his now waterless hookah. Neither of them has ever experienced a desert rainstorm that lasted forty days and nights. They certainly have never taken a cruise in their backyard desert. But Noah, like all sailors, even today, is the kind of optimist that expects to win the lottery without buying a ticket.

Spirited questions arise, what did God mean by frolicking animal pairs as 'happy-go-lucky' shipmates? And did He really suggest finger painting activities as fulfilling entertainment during this extended aimless journey? You can only finger paint and beat rocks for so long and the novelty wears off. What about special diets? Suppose our 'happy-go-luckies' get sea sick. All great questions. Sarah and Noah begin reminiscing on the days of yore when people spent their leisure time merrily killing each other and then partying while God and Goddess in their heaven took it all in good stride. Those days are now fast becoming the good ole days.

The energized Noah again speaks up. "Please God, explain this ark thing and how am I supposed to build it? Even if I could figure it out, I still have this very sore back and only a few good tools, mostly used for shodding camel's hoofs."

"Worse than that God, Noah has a lazy streak a cubit long. Getting him out of bed is my biggest daily chore. All I can say to you God is - good luck with Noah's ark building task." Sarah ends her sarcastic remarks with a sneer and a haughty snort, leaves the tent in a huff and begins softly stroking and comforting her trembling and mortified camels, who are scared out of their wits having heard God's watery scenario.

God. "Ok, Ok, settle down you two happy love birds, soon to be first time arkers. Sarah, please come back in here. I have detailed boat-building plans that I will provide Noe. All he has to do is follow them and his ark will be a nautical masterpiece. Sarah, you will be so proud of him. Since there is little, thank Me God, mathematics involved in this task, it should be easy for your devoted husband to follow and make you proud."

Noah, although enthusiastic, begins to worry. "God, you must know I can't read that Arabic numeral stuff, and I didn't even take developmental math, let alone flunk it, like You. But since I am artistic perhaps I can follow a drawing, so maybe it will work out"

"Just a minute God, before you two get engrossed in any hi-tech ark engineering issues, first - please explain to me your Ka-Boom theory and secondly is Your Nuevo drowning nightmare proposal just a subterfuge to cover up problems resulting from misbehaving creatures taking a dump in your heavens or - is it Your bad math?" Asks the still fully charged up nomad homemaker winner Sarah, who really never did like water or math.

God ignores her convoluted comments and twisted question by turning to Noah. "Good boy, ole buddy Noe." Replies God as he senses Noah is now finally taking ownership of the ark-building task. God knows full well that give a guy a boat to build - he is happy, math or no math. Sarah is a much tougher concern to be dealt with - later.

"God, you mentioned billeting pairs of animals on Noah's as yet imaginary ark. Would you please elaborate on this topic?" Continues the rebuffed but worldly wise Sarah.

"Indeed, I can. What we, no, I mean what you two have to do, is simply select pairs of healthy compatible animals, good eyes and teeth. By pairs I mean a male and a female entering their prime reproductive years, load them on the ark before the rains come." Explains God hurriedly, realizing full well that His brief explanation is in no way going to satisfy Sarah's query.

Suddenly Noah takes an interested in this topic. "Hey, God, how do we determine if the animals are male or female? I never had Sex Ed in school, but I am surely willing to learn, you know, ha, ha. Sounds like fun."

God foresees a serious and provocative talk coming up about the "birds and bees". He had not anticipated this and is certainly not prepared, but decides to wing it. "Well, ole buddy Noe, I would suggest that you first grab the animal as best you can and then go to its backside and raise its tail. Take a quick but good peek at what you see and make a scientific determination, male or female. Should be a no brainer."

"Hallelujah God Almighty, this sounds like really great fun!" blurts out a beaming Noah who hasn't a clue what he is up against.

"You licentious old pervert Noah; you will do no such thing. I will perform the sexual examinations and you, ole geezer, will build the ark. Is that clearly understood?" States Sarah vigorously. "My birthday gift certificate for you was to take a '*Train Your Brain*' course, but I will now exchange it for one on how to '*Mop Up Your Morals*.'"

This vigorous outburst by sexually conservative Sarah was about to conclude the group discussion on techniques for selecting animal pairs, until it further dawns on Noah that these examinations would be somewhat tricky to perform on flying and creeping things, like vultures, bats and vipers.

"Yeah God, how do you determine the sex of eagles, alligators, boas and the like?" Inquires Noah. "Specifically, I am wondering what might be the reaction of any self respecting serpent when I sneak a peek up its backside during its nappy time."

"Noah, you seem to have not heard what I said, or are you purposely ignoring me as you are prone to do. You will build the ark and I will "sex" the passengers, is that now clearly understood or do you again need more drawings? You really must get some professional counseling and take that extension course I suggested on acceptable behavior towards our fellow animals." Responds Sarah firmly yet compassionately.

God sees a need to quickly take charge. "Sarah, I am sure your dear Noah understands his assigned responsibilities in this historic ark project, but his natural curiosity is ever so praiseworthy. Since I have not performed these rear-end examinations myself, I am truly unable to tell you clearly what the usually independent thinking animals reaction will be, as a male I can only guess. Furthermore dear Sarah, I am sure Noe, is most relieved to know you will perform these tricky assessments. Right Noe?"

"You damn right God" replies a chuckling smirking Noah; this should be another fun packed activity prior to the upcoming cruise. "A-sailing we will go, ho, ho."

God authoritatively presses on. "Following the selection of animal pairs, you Sarah must also insure that after the waters recede, these hot to trot animals again begin making whoopee and replenish the earth with their offspring. I know you do not have a valid Marriage and Family Counseling certificate, but do your best to find compatible and loving animal pairs and then instruct them on safe sex and parenting skills while a-sea. You know what I mean, Sarah. Women are by nature good at this, right?"

Noah turns his face and allows himself a secret smile, no, a big smirk, thinking, ya right God, ole buddy. Your track record on this topic hasn't been all that stellar since your designer fig leafs went out of style.

Sarah is beginning to wonder if she should have refrained from calling Noah a pervert. Accepting the daunting task of finding compatible animal pairs to repopulate the world is not trivial; hours of animal counseling across language barriers will be challenging. Sarah now realizes that she needs to learn to keep her mouth shut in the future. Noah is really a good guy and I am going to need his expertise in these matters.

Noah is clearly energized and eager to get on with building an ark. "You can count on us God, I'll build you the biggest God darn, oops, ark there ever was and Sarah will fill it two by two of the finest ready to make whoopee animals there are in this here arid desert. We will make You proud for having masterminded this Big Drown caper.

But I have yet another question, what about the plants or will they all simply turn to seaweed?" Noah further needles God. "Do plants have a back side that needs checking, should it become necessary to put them, two by two, in the ark?"

That had never occurred to Me, thinks God, "Noe, you have an inquiring mind and presented Me with yet another provocative question. I admit that, I too, wonder if this evolutionary thing allows that to happen. Perhaps these same plants, after becoming seaweeds will later revert back to land plants. I hope to God – shucks there I go taking My own name in vain again – but for your sake Noe, we also don't want to worry about finding compatible pairs of slugs – they never presented any problems in our Garden of Eden. Golly gee, this is just another bio-genetic developmental mathematics issue that I cannot fully comprehend. How could this seemingly capricious evolutionary activity happen right under My very sensitive nose?"

Sarah. "Knock it off dear degenerate husband or you will be sleeping solo out in the scorpion infested sand dunes tonight. I am certain God has a lot on his mind right now and doesn't need sexual heckling from the likes of you."

Discussion after discussion follow into the late afternoon, from the urbane to sublime, practical to frivolous as well as godly to ungodly. It is a grueling day for all.

God is showing fatigue, while Noah is fired up. "You know dear folks; we still have a few days before the deluge so I suggest we take a much deserved break until tomorrow. I am certain you two have lots to talk about tonight. And I need to return to my Goddess and share with Her what we have accomplished today. Knowing Her, she may give Me a completely new set of directives, in which case we will have to start all over tomorrow. In addition, since Noe is a non-reader I still have to draw plans for the ark. So let us call it a day."

"Please, just another minute, God Almighty. I would surely like to meet Your Goddess. Following today's discussions I think we females probably have a lot to share that would lead to a more successful cruise. Do you think she would do lunch with me someday, before the showers begin, that is?" Pleads Sarah.

"Great idea Sare, I will ask Her. As you would expect Her daily social calendar is usually quiet full. She has so many philanthropic foundations vying for Her favors that it keeps Her occupied. For example, lately the 'Asps for Peace Freedom Fighters' has become a major time consumer for the Goddess. They are currently in need of improved fang sharpeners so they can begin some kind of asp political party promotion - a highly conservative bunch seeking deep pockets, if you know what I mean.

See ya all tomorrow."

Poof – God is gone as quickly as He had appeared earlier, leaving Sarah and Noah to decipher the unnerving and tangled pieces of God's information about a boding calamity while also trying to calm their restless camels outside. Poor things.

"My God Lady Sarah, what was all that about?" Asks Noah as he kicks off his dusty sandals and scrounges for a beer. "Seems like only yesterday I was serenely looking at local falcons as they gracefully soared above our dunes, and now it looks like everyone is up for a drowning. How can things change so fast?"

"Well, I surely don't know, 'Noe ole buddy', but I did learn some interesting things about your heretofore never discussed prurient interests in the backsides of animals. You must see a board certified psychiatrist about these unsavory interests after the cruise; I am certain they have a proper term, along with some cures and pills for this most embarrassing problem." Responds Sarah as she nervously looks at Noah.

"Gosh gee Sare, I was only trying to help you and God get a better understanding of this two-by-two thing. As the future Captain of a yet un-built ark it is my commissioned duty to insure that the crew is the best we can get when the surf is up here in our soon erstwhile Dustville." Noah squats heavily on his threadbare rug - beer in one hand and his chin cupped in the other. Discordant thoughts flash through his mind, none of them, especially the water front activities, making any sense to a lifetime bona fide landlubber who had never seen a god, let alone discussed an upcoming catastrophe.

"While you relax and sip your beer I'll scurry up a goat grab for dinner." Quips Sarah. "May as well start eating some goats since only two of them can go a-cruising."

"Good thinking Sarah." Chimes Noah who is quietly guzzling his warm beer hoping the stresses of the day will soon begin fading. "Your goat a-day menu is fine with me."

CHAPTER 3

HEAVENLY CONVERSATIONS

God wearily drags himself up into heaven, greets his Goddess with a quick peck on her right cheek. He then collapses on a soft fluffy cumulus nimbus cloud. Goddess smiles lovingly and cheerfully asks God how his early morning encounter with Noah and Sarah went.

"My dear beautiful poopsie Goddess lollypop; thank God I am not a short fused God prone to cursing and violent behavior, but I tell you straight out baby, today was a challenge. Frankly I am not sure this flood and drown concept is going to solve anything. I know We wish to clean up the evolutionary chaos that has occurred but I am truly concerned that the progeny of Sarah, Noah and their seafaring menagerie may not improve matters. I personally really need some Jack and diet seven tonight." pleads a despondent God.

Like Noah, God kicks off his sandals and stretches out, waiting for the bourbon and diet seven to take off the day's rough edges. "I have just got to learn more mathematics to get on top of this genetic mutation probability mess. Goddess, where did you put my first grade remedial arithmetic primer?"

"My dear God poopkins, You just relax now after such a trying day, enjoy Your drink while I fix dinner. Your math book is around here somewhere, but let it go for tonight. Just wait and see what I have cooked up for dessert tonight. While You are relaxing on your cloud nine you might just take a peek at …."

Goddess is suddenly interrupted by God's screaming at Her "Stop it Goddess lollypop, I have been up to My yoo-hoo in peeking talk all day and can't stand hearing that word again."

An extended period of silence ensues, broken only by the occasional slurping sound of God's drinking and the clinking of ice cubes. The Goddess is stunned, wondering what God's robust outburst about peeking is all about?

"Sorry I blew up Goddess, but all day Sarah and Noah were at it talking about peeking up backsides of wild animals to determine their sex. Then I had to explain making whoopee, which is substantially different from Immaculate Conception, right?" responds, a cranky God, who was looking forward to getting a buzz as soon as possible. At this moment God has no desire to rehash the day on the desert in Noah and Sarah's tent.

"Hold it right there buster God. What is this dirty talk about peeking up the bum sides of animals? After all these years have You now turned into a peeking God? Moreover, what is up with this making whoopee?" The Goddess is completely taken aback by all this kind of un-Godly talk. "As I now recall We worked through this delicate topic when We chased everyone out of the Garden sans fig leaves.

"I thought I had problems with My apple pie today, but You have now brought another more insidious problem into our happy little universe." Goddess is clearly distraught and somewhat intentionally spills God's private 12 year reserve bottle of Jack all over their personal cosmic cloud.

"Please, please poopsie Goddess lollypop just let Me drown - sorry - bad choice of words; My troubles today are overwhelming Me. I will elaborate on backsides and whoopee later on." pleads God, wondering why He ever created sex to begin with. What was I thinking?

"OK, poopkins You are off the hook, but only for the moment. This topic needs in depth exploring and for sure I now have no second doubts about flooding this God (oops) forsaken desert. You will notice I said God forsaken and not Goddess forsaken. Drink up Chum!"

"Thanks lollypop, You are just too good to Me. What would I do without You?" Says the now smiling and mellowing God, as the smooth spirits softly trickle down His throat and softens thoughts throughout His cerebrum and cerebellum.

"Skoal, my dear poopkins." Quips Goddess from the kitchen as She sips Her gin and tonic and goes back to the business of pots, pans and preparing a scrumptious just heavenly meal.

The Goddess and God are elegantly seated for dinner, toasting and sipping a nice merlot. Dinner harp music is playing softly in the background as They dreamily look into each other's eyes. God suddenly observes that the Goddess has fixed a luscious rump roast for dinner. He chokes, spewing Jack everywhere.

Goddess. "Dear God, dear poopkins, what is the matter? Doesn't that rump roast just smell heavenly tonight? I shopped all morning to find the best cut and then marinated it for several hours before putting it in the oven. Why don't You now deftly carve it so We can savor its flavor?"

God has instantly lost his appetite and almost His will to go on living. Of all the entrées lollypop Goddess could have fixed for tonight, She had selected rump roast. God cannot believe His run of bad luck this day. Being God is a thankless job with constant unprovoked irritations, I must rise above them.

"Oh, my dear, dear Goddess, yes You have such a beautiful rump, I mean roast, and it smells so scrumptious. How in the universe can I ever thank You for this outstanding dining experience?" Responds God realizing He is improving at unabashed gibberish and lying.

The bewildered Goddess isn't sure just what God is talking about, Her juicy dinner rump roast or Her well endowed derrière, which He has never before commented on and surely never mentioned that it smelled good. Quickly She pours herself another full glass of wine, still confused while trying to figure out the meaning of God's remarks.

The Goddess and God continue dining informally but quietly. Heavenly harps are now playing wild country swing in the background, interspersed with claps of thunder and flashing bolts of bright lightning. While God continues to savor His rump roast He is simultaneously swilling down one bottle of red wine after another in good ole college chug-a-lug fashion. Finally, their dinner is over and God asks the Goddess what kind of after dinner drink she would enjoy.

"A triple shot of Portuguese port, please." Coos the Goddess. "And fix a double cognac for Yourself. We earned it today."

Celestial calm settles in as God's spiraling galaxies swirl about silently, while black holes continue sucking up dead stars and stellar debris. It is truly a heavenly scene. Finally the distant thunder is replaced by stillness, interrupted occasionally by deep guttural groans from a dying red giant in some far away distant corner of the universe.

It had been a full day for the God and Goddess as it had for Noah and Sarah. All greatly deserved and needed a good night's sleep in order to begin a new day fully refreshed to continue preparation for the impending rainy season.

CHAPTER 4

DAY ONE

God and Goddess wake up lazily after a good nights respite and cheerfully greet another heavenly new day. God is eager to get on with Noah's ark-building project and then begin the monsoon season. He gives the Goddess a peck on Her rosy cheeks and dashes straight down to Noah and Sarah's humble, now thoroughly cleaned up tent. He remembers not to comment on Sarah's dusty floor. Again with pomp and gusto He enthusiastically bursts in with a cheery ta-ta – "I am here to greet the day with you."

Sarah greets God with anything but a cheery ta-ta greeting. Big dark bags droop heavily beneath her tear stained blood shot red eyes. Her old badly stained coffee pot is noisily boiling over while she incoherently mumbles to herself something about here comes ole joy-boy God himself.

"Hi there Sare, How goes it with you love birds on this glorious top of the mornin' day?" Chirps the smiling God hoping things will go well today.

"God, you don't want to know, and please knock off the ta-ta, tally ho ho chatter." retorts a very tired and distraught Sarah. God is somewhat shaken by Sarah's appearance and dower demeanor.

"Dear God" replies God. "What, in this soon to be submerged world of yours is the matter, Sarah? And what's with Noe over there in the corner - seemingly dead?"

"Oh, yeah God, Noah should be dead, but so far he and the rest of us are not that lucky, but I think we are getting closer."

"Pray tell me what happened Sarah. Maybe ole God here can make it better."

Sarah sniffles a haughty response. "That's a joke God. As you yourself admitted yesterday, You and Your missus could not fix the Big Ka-Boom fiasco that You started years ago. So to solve that unsolvable problem You think – no - no - You guess – that a monsoonal rainstorm will improve on Your ever evolving disastrous predicament. You surely must be joshing about making life better through drowning. Quite a provocative slogan we now have: 'Better living through drowning.' How did You ever come up with such an off the wall idea? You may need a new pr firm to sell the concept."

Sarah stares directly at God and continues. "Your problem with the universe is your problem, but the more immediate issue for me is my dear, nigh onto death, husband Noah. Last night after your dire revelations Noah felt the need to tie on a real doozer and then wandered over to our neighbor Mustafa's tent and blabbed all Your plans, including aft end examinations of all animals before drowning all but two. Needless to say Mustafa was also not thrilled by this future. Then, as You would expect from a couple of drunken demented males, they continued lascivious gender talk about birds."

"Oh, No!" Exclaims God, realizing this may again be another challenging day.

"Oh Yeah. Now Mustafa, our so-so neighbor for many years has this mean old falcon, which was quietly roosting in the tent minding its own business, judiciously picking fleas, during Noah's oration on how to determine the sex of birds of prey. Noah then abruptly decides he is going to demonstrate to Mustafa the gender of his award winning falcon. As I understand it, based on your instructions God, Noah goes over and using his left hand lovingly pets Mustafa's falcon on its forehead, thinking that will curry his good nature. Well, we now know for sure that this clever diversionary maneuver does not work." Sarah draws a deep breath and continues.

"What follows is somewhat confusing, but I gather my idiot Noah while petting the falcon with his left hand, takes his right hand and begins checking out the falcon's rear end feathers. In a nanosecond or less, Noah has lost an eye ball and his upper torso is scratched beyond recognition. He comes running, screaming and bleeding home. I did try to patch him up before he collapsed in a bloody drunken heap over there." Sarah's voice is weak and she has begun to whimper. "I worry he will die, I love him so much."

"Oh, no, no, may heaven help us all." gasps the deeply moved God as He reassuringly cuddles Sarah. "You know I can fix that dying thing, so please don't worry."

"Aye God, thank you. But while You are here getting ready to drown us with a major misguided shower what heavenly whiz-bang is running heaven and the rest of Your cosmic run amok stuff You complained about? I worry we have not seen the end of this deadly frivolity and that there is more calamity to come. Who is in charge?" snaps a now fully hysterical Sarah. She has good reasons; her husband lies dying, her world is about to be drowned and all the while mutations are proliferating totally out of control.

There is a loud gassy burp from Noah who had earlier crawled under a blanket. Stirring motions follow and a wobbly pitiful Noah arises. God notes that indeed his left eye is missing; his face and upper body are covered with massive deep wounds still oozing fresh blood. However, as always, Noah puts on a farcical happy face.

"Top of the mornin, as you said God. How are You and the Missus on this beautiful sun shiny day?"

Noah continues. "God, You should have been here last night. It was a hoot. After a couple of beers I thought I would share our future grandiose plans with Mustafa about what You said was going to happen. Ha-ha. That neighborly gesture only cost me one eye, a couple of liters of blood and the friendship of my now erstwhile pal Mustafa. He may never see his prizewinning nasty grumpy falcon again, but, at least we determined its gender. Guess what? Mustafa and I decided that his old bird must be a female. Wouldn't you know it?" Noah told all this without a sense of rancor or anger, indeed he seemed proud of himself.

Sarah. "Noah, you inveterate liar, you had consumed two six packs before kicking off this badly conceived avian physical examination and you really do not have a clue as to what happened. I am committing you into a research rescue center where they study nincompoops like you in the name of science. Furthermore I thought we were all sworn to secrecy of this impending big time shower. What happened to security?"

God is reeling, but He is getting used to it, He now tries to pour more smooth talk on the volatile situation. "Well, you know what Noe? Mustafa and others in the neighborhood would naturally begin asking penetrating questions as your ark building progresses here among the dunes. An ark rising in the desert might draw some curiosity, don't you think? Not to worry. Noe. Your construction site will eventually invoke applause as it majestically rises towards the heavens. Of course it may also confound a few as how truly out of place this thing seems to be, but I have a hunch they will simply chalk it up to your well established idiosyncrasies and go on with their miserable lives. Some may even chuckle a bit at your seemingly stupid behavior, ha-ha. Little do they know that you will have the last laugh. Good clean humor is always healthy. But more importantly Noe, what in the world are you going to do about your missing eyeball and all the scars that will result from your non-routine falcon examination?"

Eternally upbeat Noah replies cheerfully. "God, You know this entire incident is turning out to be a godsend, no offense. I have been thinking that I will get a designer black one-eye patch to give me a real sea dog pirate appearance. The deep scars add further testimony to my past fighting escapades. I promise not to tell anyone that they resulted from sexually examining an overly sensitive upset old female falcon. All this toughness will stand me in good stead when we take to sea, aye mates? As for the ridicule bestowed on me by my neighbor sand bangers, not to fret, their derisive attitude will turn to envy as we sail away and they are up to their knickers in a rising sea."

Sarah does not know whether to continue crying or simply go blind to stop the tears, so she starts laughing while hysterically yelling, "Man the life boats, man the life boats, I am getting the hell off this un-built ark crewed by lunatics."

However, in the end God and Sarah are both deeply impressed, as they see standing before them a wobbly, hung over, potential naval commodore and future hero. Shaky as Noah's stance is, he is exuding a truly hung over naval officer's demeanor. Sarah's tears dry and she now beams with pride knowing she is so fortunate to have a gifted nautically endowed sailor husband. Noah, a man who has never seen an ark nor an ocean, but by golly looks like a badly beat-up swaggering one-eyed swashbuckler is now on the verge of becoming the ultimate desert buffoon, while saving two by two pairs, of animals. Sarah realizes this is high desert drama, but still wonders what am I doing in this no-win water show?

"Ok, Ok," Cheers God as He begins to sense that His and the Goddess's deluge program is finally underway, albeit with a one-eyed captain and his skeptical sassy wife. "You know mates; I am beginning to experience the same thrill I had before We set off the Big KaBoom. I wish the Goddess were here to share with us this momentous moment. Here are your final visual ark plans Noe, I worked till early dawn getting them ready and proofed. Build a big rugged ark that will make us all proud, as you save your, Sarah's and your cruising menagerie's derrieres from a premature watery demise." God smartly throws Noah a nautical salute.

"Aye, Aye God." respond Sarah and Noah in unison returning God's snappy sailor's salute. The saluting customs of ancient arkers are indeed regal and they continue today only but with more pomp.

CHAPTER 5

ARK BUILDING

Noah was emotionally fully recovered from his encounter with Mustafa's falcon, but the upset raptor had flown his desert tent coop and did not return which rankled Mustafa to the point where he daily starts making smart-alec remarks about Noah's strange looking construction. Just where does he think he will get an ocean to float it in? "What disappoints me the most Noah, my former best neighbor, is that my precious falcon is not here to sit on my shoulder and enjoy your unraveling sanity and your entertaining insanity. Perhaps she would even take a whack at your other eye, eh?" Chides Mustafa.

Despite Mustafa's caustic remarks, the ark building continues in full swing. Huge trees from far away mountain tops are dragged by nervous camels to the valley where Noah saws them into heavy planks. Turns out that Noah has many little unknown innate skills, as well as exuberance for ark building. Finally, after great efforts a magnificent ark rises majestically between the sand dunes in front of Sarah and Noah's tent. God drops in periodically and proudly approves of Noah's gargantuan efforts. Mustafa continues his endless mean spirited heckling while grieving deeply for his missing prized falcon. Noah has mixed guilt feelings here. The falcon was mean, but Noah should not have publicly embarrassed her right to personal privacy. "I am really sorry."

Sarah and the Goddess have become close friends, sharing camel burger lunches with exquisite desert date wines on an almost daily basis. The Goddess always graciously picks up the tab and leaves a generous tip. The two develop a deep camaraderie, seldom if ever, witnessed among Godly and un-Godly females. Basically an oxymoron.

Sarah begins to share her concerns for properly taking care of the ark's passengers. "You know Goddess, Noah and I are going to be faced with a plethora of housekeeping and psychological problems when all these assorted animals, two by two, get on board. You know each animal evolved differently through natural selection and all that stuff. As a result each has developed unique behavior and communication patterns. It is going to be a challenge to keep them gainfully occupied while we gaily sail around waiting for everyone else to drown. Any suggestions, Goddess?"

"You'll figure it out, Sare." consoles the Goddess, Who loves dispensing heavenly advice. "Maybe they would enjoy some outdoor on deck activities like playing: drop the hanky, pinning a tail on the donkey, bobbing for apples, four legged hop scotch, snake hissing contests, rock climbing and the like. The key is to keep their minds off of making whoopee while at sea or you will end up with an overpopulated maternity ward in the ark. On the other hand, they do need to develop some social skills so that they do not end up nasty and inconsiderate towards each other when they get back on land. By all means stay away from adult games."

"What do you suggest I do about dining arrangements Goddess? You know many of these animals are used to eating each other as a regular diet. I suppose Noah can try to get some hay and see if we can get the lions, tigers, et al to go vegan. However, if their protein consumption habits are not solved by them converting to healthy vegetables we could end up with an ark full of empty stinking carcasses. Not a festive dining thought." The discussion on planning for daily chores during the cruise is beginning to tire Sarah while the Goddess is equally clueless, so they change the subject to debating essences of French perfumes.

Noah is on a roll. The ark construction is moving ahead of schedule and without cost overruns. Since Noah is oblivious of mathematics he doesn't have to take seriously displacement factors, keel weight, and rudder extension linkages to the pilothouse, which he calls his bridge. The vessel takes on the appearance of a disfigured Rube Goldberg creation, greatly entertaining Mustafa and his dusty nomad buddies. They arrive early and stay late developing a great sense of bad humor at Noah's expense.

Noah has to worry about the billeting of this animal kingdom so they won't all bunch together on one side or the other of his ark. This means building pens, sties, stalls, cages, corals and fences. With a black patch over the spot where is left eye use to be, Noah forges on without depth perception. God is mighty proud and is now bringing Noah cool beers to keep the pace apace. Every afternoon at about one PM they begin their happy hour, followed by philosophizing and occasionally addressing engineering challenges. Since neither one is particularly adept at engineering, solutions to the construction issues boil down to by guess and by golly. In spite of these random like decisions the ark surely looks nautical.

Finally one night shortly after midnight, there is a brilliant flash of light followed immediately by an ear shattering clap of rolling thunder that shakes every tent, camel and camel driver in the neighborhood. Sarah and Noah leap out of bed as they hear a few soft pitty-patters of rain bouncing on their tent. "It has started!" yells a jubilant Noah. "Hallelujah, where is my black eye patch and captain's cap. This is it mates, ship ahoy."

"Now what?" Is all a sleepy, nonplussed Sarah can muster in response to the loud commotion outside. She briefly stands up but quickly returns to bed hoping it will all disappear and she can continue her snooze. Noah is elated by this racket, as are all arker/sailors when caught in a thunderstorm.

God appears with a full grin showing His pearly white teeth that literally sparkle enough to light up Noah's tent. "How about that gang? This is just a taste of things to come. It was a good show, eh? I hope you both enjoyed My prelude to the big event. I will now shut it off."

Sarah, now fully awake, screams back, "You stupid male idiots, Noah doesn't have the tub – excuse meee – 'THE ARK' even half finished, I don't have all the animals sexed and corralled while you God Almighty get your jollies by scaring the living bejesus out of the neighborhood. You dolts are creating a disaster before the disaster. I again quit. The two of you can go to that other special place that You God also created or maybe You would rather sail off into the sunset with all Your animals bent on making whoopee, without me." Sarah rolls over in a fetal position, hunkers down under her blanket pouting and whimpering as though mortally wounded. "Why, oh why me Lord?"

God and Noah are understandably speechless by Sarah's somewhat hostile comments, but are enjoying the sweet aroma of a soft shower in the desert in the middle of the night. It smells and feels so good. They agree, it was a delightful prelude of things to come. It is definitely a half full glass situation, thinks Noah.

However, while Sarah's adrenalin is still raging; she abruptly throws aside her blanket and continues. "The Goddess and I have been having some serious discussions while enjoying our daily lunches. She said that the Big KaBang idea was God's not Hers, and now we have to drown everyone to undo this monumental cosmic booboo. We agreed that you males always gravitate to big bang ideas. This damn phony thunder and lightning show of yours God is another example of just how you stupid males try to solve big problems with big noises, and then think you are ever so cute at the same time. Jeesus, oops, he hasn't yet arrived, has he? I am going back to sleep and you two bone heads better come up with better ideas by morning. Good night, or is it good bye guys? By the way we are all out of beer, ha, ha, serves you right."

God begins to regret having stopped His little teaser shower. I should have let the damn thing run and drowned out the entire bunch of ungrateful creatures right here and now.

Noah. "Oh God, it is OK, you know how females tend to get a bit cheeky when woken from a Prince Charming dream, just after the frog encounter. As we have witnessed before, Sarah will be OK in the morning when she again gets to brewing her daily coffee. Let us call it a night. They shake, separate and everyone drifts off into a nightmarish sleep full of wet dreams.

Next morning God sheepishly drops in on Noah. "God, I am having serious troubles with the ark. Since the timber is green the planking has begun to shrink meaning there will be a gazillion leaks once the waters rise. That means every creature in the lower decks will naturally scramble to get topside. If they all end up on the same side of the ark we could become the first desert Vassa ark capsize in history. Then what? Are we stuck treading ocean until the ark sinks or do You have some other nifty scheme for saving animal life - on a selectively limited scale of course? We have not discussed life arks or dinghies. For example are we going to need life preservers for hippos and elephants? I need answers."

"Right Noe; this cargo instability potential isn't a reassuring situation, is it? But trust Me, you won't need life rafts. By the way the Goddess also gave Me the dickens following that sudden sprinkle last night. Apparently the increase in humidity undid some of Her recent curls. I really thought it was a capital idea to give everyone in the desert some experience for the real thing." Said a dejected God, while being reminded that planning for the future is often futile, as witnessed by all His prior creations.

God continues musing out loud. "You know it has not been to our mutual advantage that the Goddess and Sarah have been doing lunches these past weeks. They probably sit and gossip about how bad things are getting with the prospect of getting worse. I tell you straight out Noe, we have some serious problems facing us and the least one may not be the rainy season. Truly, I am having second thoughts about this deluge. What if the water isn't deep enough and there are renegade survivors?"

Noah. "Sorry to hear this ole Buddy God. You are right; personnel problems often get in the way of progress, especially a massive drowning. While we can surely handle the naval ark architectural challenges, personality quirks and idiosyncrasies may sink our yet un-launched ark. You know what, God? Pouty lips sink arks."

"Furthermore, You just alluded to the fact that if the rains aren't sufficient this caper may also become a bust. Does that then mean we may be bobbing around on a body of fresh rain water with perhaps habited sand dune islands surrounding us? Good grief."

"What to do Noe? If I call this high profile caper off, we will all become the laughing stock of the desert and maybe the universe. A new generation of wars to end all wars will begin anew. My Godly credibility rating is again at stake – dung. Think of all the embarrassing jokes people will make up about who stopped God's deluge or was it a miscalculation? My heavenly tasks are not trivial." Laments God looking out to the heavens wondering what his Goddess is fixing for dinner.

"Well God, if You are worried about your dinner, you can always join Sarah and me, we are still busily gnawing away on goats that won't make the final cut."

God. "Thanks ole buddy, but my Goddess is expecting me. And luckily We are finally running out of rump roasts. What would I do without you Noe? Ciao."

CHAPTER 6

THE CRUISE

The morning of the long anticipated big event dawns steel grey with a softly falling mist. Noah's tent is covered with heavy dew. The smell in the air definitely forecasts rain. However, God had earlier learned his lesson and would not let this, the real thing, come upon Noah with surprise. Sarah is fixing what would be her last pot of home brew coffee on a dry terra firma for an unknown period of time. Noah has fired up his hookah, his black eye patch is in place and he is eagerly, but nervously, looking forward to going to sea. Outside their tent Mustafa is making his usual ridiculing remarks about constructing an ark in the desert.

The rainy season now begins in earnest. It will continue relentlessly for exactly forty days and nights. At first the sand can absorb the water, but as the sand becomes saturated the rain water will build to a sea. Mustafa's perch has moved up on the dunes.

Sarah hands Noah his cup of hot dark coffee and with a sigh of sadness in her voice; "Drink up my dear Noah, This could be the last cup of my homemade coffee you get for a long, like a really long time, unless we can figure out how to make it on ark-board."

Unnoticed Big Guy God has entered the tent and with a winsome smile, lovingly puts His arms around Noah and Sarah thanking them profusely for a job very well done. "This has not been an easy task for any of us, but you two have been exemplar. As I came over, I noticed the graceful lines of the ark's hull and the magnificent bulging upper and lower structures designed to hold the animals, two by two.

And that monstrous bridge on top makes a statement even if looks a bit like a flying outhouse. You two are in for a fantastic cruise."

"As I later walked alongside the ark among the cages and pens of loving animals I could see how perfectly you Sarah paired them; some were already intensely eyeing each other with teen age puppy love, tee-hee. So, the time is now, get your passengers on board and I will crank up the showers. In a few short days you will be merrily at sea. I also noticed that Mustafa's heckling comments have an unusual caustic bite to them this morning."

"Hallelujah God Almighty, we are ready to go to sea. I just can't wait. Come on Sarah; let's get the animals on board." Shouts the ever excitable Noah while adjusting his eye patch and snappy arky cap.

"You know I am curious Sare, how did you work out the feeding routine so that the big animals don't consume the smaller ones? If that were to happen, I suppose there is the chance that you and Noe would end up looking at two tigers, eye ball to eye ball, on what would become your last day at sea. This would certainly defeat our overall mission, wouldn't it?" Inquires God, acknowledging the possibility of yet another failure.

"Oh, you old silly God, the Goddess and I came up with this ingenious mess plan. We are going to make every animal a vegetarian. We have filled the boat, excuse me ark, with tons of hay and rutabagas. All the animals will eat hay for roughage and rutabagas for vitamins and minerals. How about that for a healthy nutritious cuisine while at sea?" Boasts Sarah.

Wow, thinks God, this dining will be most interesting to observe – from afar. Panthers, hyenas, snakes and the like all eating straw and rutabagas, my, oh, my. However it certainly is the kind of diet the Goddess would approve – especially the lo-cal part. God meekly ventures a question, "Where in the world did you find rutabagas, what are they, and are they easy to come by here in the desert? They must be another one of those flora mutations I don't understand."

Sarah, "We had to go to a burg called Askov to get them. Not an easy task either, since rutabagas had to be plucked out among piles of lookalike glacial rocks. Extremely rare plant, God – hard to chew - but good."

The rain now increases in intensity, accompanied by vicious gusts of cold wind adding to the misery.

God does not want to participate in any teary eyed fare-thee-well bon voyage ceremony and is about to leave when Sarah inquires, "Where is the Goddess, isn't She going to see us off? She told me at lunch yesterday, She couldn't wait for us to get arking."

Noah is getting antsy, "I am going to begin billeting passengers; we must move fast!" The rain is falling heavier accompanied with near gale strength winds that make life outdoors brutally unpleasant. Noah and Sarah's tent is flapping wildly and a corner is partially submerged. Many animals are shivering while standing in cold water. Noah's trusty and now forlorn camels are a pitiful sight as they try to maintain their regal demeanor while hip deep in rainwater and understandably nervous about their future.

"Slow down, Captain, first we must give all the animals a potty break. This is going to be a long journey and best we start out on empty." Admonishes Sarah, ever sensitive to animal's inner physical as well as psychological needs. "You take the big animals around back of the ark and I will take care of the smaller gentler ones on the lee side."

"By the by and by God, just where is the Goddess? Surely She is going to see us go to sea?" inquires Sarah a second time. She feels the need to hug her regular luncheon friend, gossiper and bosom confidant.

"I am sorry to say Sarah that my Goddess woke up with a really nasty backache this morning. She has been having lots of them lately. Furthermore, She had Her hair done yesterday, a big up-do-do bouffant and when She saw the drizzle She decided to stay in Her snug dry bed in heaven, for Her hair's sake. But, She did ask Me to wish you a most successful voyage and She will definitely take you to lunch when the sea sinks. She knew you would understand Her predicament. Happy arking – Ta-ta." God is gone in a puff as the rain, thunder and lightning increase dramatically. Truly a Ben-Hur epic moment.

The rain keeps falling relentlessly and this is only day one. Sarah is deeply hurt by the Goddess's failure to show, and especially the lame excuse of it being due to a bad hair day. Sarah begins wondering if the Goddess is simply a fair weather friend not to be counted on in a shower. No female takes these kinds of excuses well or lightly.

First time arker/boater Noah, his stressed out wife Sarah and their yakking, crowing, meowing, hissing, bellowing menagerie, standing in the mud waiting turns to empty bladders, are all dumb founded, looking at each other wondering what in the world lies before them, and more importantly what did they do wrong to deserve this kind of attention. Noah carefully adjusts his eye patch thinking to himself. "So this is how cruises begin - everyone peeing in the sand – wow."

In the slippery soggy mud Noah and Sarah continue boarding the animals, two by two. This is not an easy task, as the winds are approaching hurricane category two force, accompanied by streaks of lightning and thunderclaps that scare the dickens out of the animals. The stench from the wet animals and their final land deposits adds a real down to earth touch to the misery. Finally the boarding task is completed. "All present and accounted for." Yells Sarah over the howling wind. Captain Noah is ecstatic, but the rain has caused his eye patch to slip, giving him a bedraggled god forsaken pirate appearance. A empty bottle of rum in his right hand would have completed the picture.

The ark is loaded to the gunnels. They sit, stand, lie, fly and wait. Day after day the water rises. Day twenty passes, only twenty more to go. On the starboard side the wooden posts that prop up Noah's ark, until it floats, are straining, due to shifting cargo, and appear to be buckling. Noah begins urgently yelling to God. "Hurry up with the rain ole buddy God, before this ark topples on the leeward side where we all took our pre-departure relief breaks."

The rains remain torrential as predicted. Everyone continues hunkered down in the ark's bowels adjusting to a radically unfamiliar life style that is just beginning to unfold. From an arid environment to one of high humidity is a switch, but with many positive benefits. All the animals find their skin getting smoother and softer, less itchy. It was just so darn much fun to lick yourself, tasting the fresh cool rain water. For most this is definitely their first full body shower and they really enjoyed it. Today's sailors can identify with this luxury of a fresh water shower – after a sail, not before.

Noah possessed an innate ability to anticipate the future, which speaks well of God's decision to put him in charge during the earth's social restructuring period. Noah had, without plans or skill, built on the topside of his ark a private command area that he had named the 'bridge'. No one really knows why he used the term bridge but it lent a certain status to Noah's aerie hide away. This bridge concept seemed inspirational and has survived into modern naval times. It was another nautical break through by ark Captain Noah.

As Captain Noah steps into his newly finished windy rain swept bridge to take command he is startled to see Mustafa's crotchety old falcon perched on the helm. The falcon looks bedraggled, sad and pitiful, but has a tiny, barely recognizable smirk on his face and a nervous mischievous twitch in his beak.

"What in God's name are you doing on my ark, you miserable critter? After having hacked out my port eye and scratched deep gouges in my body you have the audacity to come aboard my ark at this critical time. Has the word leaked that you are all going to drown?" Noah is furious and wondering if Mustafa has also somehow strayed aboard.

"My dear, dear compassionate Captain of God's Majesty's Royal Navy, I came here to apologize for my inexcusable mean-spirited behavior many nights ago. The message around the tents and dunes is that you are going cruising and I just wanted to say how sorry I am before it is too late. You were always so kind and decent to me, not like my mouthy abuser owner Mustafa, who made me catch desert mice for sport. The night when you paid us a visit I was so overjoyed that someone finally showed an interest in my backside feathers that I completely lost all my self control and reverted to vile animalistic behavior. Can you find forgiveness in that big kind heart of yours for a poor wretched over-reactive senile falcon that now has no future but drowning, please?" whimpered the ever so cagey falcon, hoping to touch Noah's soft spot. "By the way Captain you look just dashing in that jabberwocky black eye patch getup."

Dang. Why am I the patsy for this flea infested ego centric chicken? Thought Noah. After a few moments of reflection, Captain Noah recovered. "You know Falc, which is now going to be your nickname; you actually did do me a favor. Today I look like a fearless scared up one eyed buccaneer. All thanks to you. But having you on this ark is going to be a problem; you are not one of God's two by two arrangements. This means you had better be unseen by God, the Goddess and my wife Sarah until we are well at sea. Is that clearly understood?"

"Aye, Aye and more ayes - my hero Captain Noah. You can count on my two keen eyes - eyes that can spot a scrawny sand mouse five miles away, in clear weather that is, - for detecting any ocean peril ahead as our ark sails on and on to nowhere. You are the bravest and most courageous arker in the whole world, and soooo generous. Oh my, oh my, how can I ever thank you enough, Sahib?" Gushed Falc, realizing Noah really is most gullible and generous.

"Stop your blubbering Falc, and don't call me Sahib, I am Captain Noah to you and that's final. Now get lost down in the bowels of my ark or I'll have you drowned. And by the way I had better not find your former master Mustafa squirreled away with you below deck or you'll both go overboard."

"Hang on Cap, I have one additional small personal favor to ask and by the way this will also be a full life time insurance policy on your remaining eye." Injects Falc.

"OK, Falc, what is this one itty-bitty special favor you seek?"

"I will at all times reside right here in your bridge. There is no way I will be cooped up in a cage below deck on this floating henhouse. We agree then?"

Falc quickly scampers away elated. He is so pleased with himself and his eloquent powers of persuasion - thinking I should become a motivational speaker for folks about to drown. But he realizes his own future remains uncertain.

From his lofty private perch, The Bridge, Noah with his deep purple scars, black eye patch over one eye and sly gleam in his remaining eye begins to give orders to ship away. The rains continue unabated until finally the ark is sort of afloat.

Thankfully Falc is nowhere to be seen. But his unannounced appearance nags Noah.

God specified no cruise destination or time of arrival to Noah, just keep the ark's passengers happy and crew enjoying the oceanic ambiance until He, God, is convinced that it is time to land and get on with whoopee. For what it is worth – and as an aside - this noble objective continues to be the modern sailor's primary excuse for going to sea.

Sarah, the sole human female on this 'once in a life time' cruise, had taken on the billeting chores. She was busy with cage, pen and sty assignments, food preparation, dining schedules, recreational activities, spiritual counseling and other miscellaneous chores that had fallen through the cracks in God and Noah's grandiose sail-away plans. No pun intended, but Noah's ark was rife with cracks, the least of which were watery leaks from unseasoned timbers.

Nourishment was also becoming a major problem. Sarah and the Goddess had wrongly guessed that all the animals would gladly become vegans, for obvious health reasons. Hay would serve as bulk and rutabagas would provide needed minerals and vitamins for sustaining good health. The ever creative Noah secretly realized that with rutabagas on board he could probably brew beer should the occasion arise. That would at least keep him nourished and in good spirits.

Sarah exhales with a deep sigh, "At least we are alive, and not doing free style breast strokes. Downside thoughts center on, how long will this cruise last? I must get off the self pity stuff and tend to the needs of all our passengers. Gee-sus. Where are the pots and pans on this scow, oops ark?" It is time to get a-cook-n, although the ark is still firmly sitting on sand. The giddiness of going to sea was getting to Sarah.

The rains remain torrential; the ark rises ever so slowly. Finally, there is a strange feeling of unfettered freedom as the ark momentarily floats free. Then its keel abruptly bumps into a submerged dune and everybody lurches forward. Cages fly all over, animals loudly lamenting they want to get out and back on land. The rains continue unabated. The ark is almost afloat, but every so often there is another jarring event resulting from hitting unseen objects below.

Sarah screams from the aft portion of the ark. "Noah, stop this bumping around. All the animals, and me, have mal de mer. Everyone is upchucking all over the place. The stench is choking us. We can't stand it anymore, now stop it! Do you hear me?"

Noah, the ultimate ark commander and chief, smiles as he enjoys the regal ambiance of command from his private bridge. "Hang in there First Mate Sarah; you and your faithful passengers will soon rise about these sunken dunes and drowning masses as we all sail freely to nowhere in particular. Just keep in mind my old pappy's saying, that in adversity lurks opportunity. Don't you just love the smell of this fresh sea air?"

"Shut the hell up" retorts Sarah. "And please do not lecture me on my colorful language - you nit wit If you think opportunity lurks in animal excrement and its accompanying aroma you have a long ways to go before you earn your admiral's license." The obnoxious methane fumes are reaching Noah's bridge and he begins sympathizing with

Sarah's tribulations. Another adage pops into Noah's mind; what goes in must come out, but he wisely keeps it to himself.

Noah was right, after a few more weeks of heavy rains the ark floats freely above all the dunes. This is a sight to behold, nothing, but nothing, except the endless sea as far as the eyes can see. Noah, though born on a sand dune and never having seen much water in one spot was in his element and becoming a true sea dog. "Isn't this just fantastic, Sarah dear? Did you ever imagine we would one day be cruising with a select passenger list like ours while the rest of the whole world is swimming about us in complete mortal panic?" Exudes visionary Captain Noah.

Sarah responds on a somewhat different note. "Get off of it. You, the God and Goddess are three of the dumbest entities I have ever known. This cruise is completely irrational. Look at all those land animals in the ocean trying to tread water alongside our smelly ark pleading to be rescued. They are slowly succumbing while here we sit on top of a floating self-made dung heap, sea sick and scared out of our wits. Now you tell me Noah, that this is not nth dimensional lunacy. It is not even bad comedy."

Shish, thinks Noah, not daring to look Sarah in the eye. Thank God, I have enough navigation and piloting problems to keep me from becoming distracted, self-centered and pitiful. I wonder why the rudder doesn't seem to turn the ark. Probably stuck.

And stuck it is. It finally dawns on Noah that his sea is full of big, like really big, fish. These are huge mean whales, the kind that earlier had scarfed down Jonah for lunch, which ironically ended up saving Jonah. Now one of these same behemoth humpbacks is stuck in Noah's ark's rudder. The whale is effectively wildly piloting Noah's ark. "Dang it!" yells Noah to Sarah. Get to the rear and shove the stuck whale away from our rudder, hurry, we are in jeopardy!"

"Noah, stop your relentless sick talk about rears, I thought we had settled that issue a long time ago. Is your obsession with rears getting worse here at sea? Good thing I know how to steer this scow. I'll stay forward and take the helm while you go aft, not rear, and play 'poke the whale'." Sarah is clearly not in a joking mood, but grudgingly goes aft to investigate the irritating whale problem.

Sarah skillfully finishes shoving and pushing away the stubborn whale; the ark is again floating unencumbered but not smoothly. As she makes her way back to the bridge she lovingly assures each and every petrified, upchucking animal that all is well with the ark. And, aren't they all happy and lucky to be alive? However, many of them are not so sure.

Captain Noah is understandably uneasy about the upcoming unannounced entrance of Mustafa's falcon and how he will introduce this nasty raptor to his unsuspecting Sarah. That moment could occur any time. What if Mustafa also shows up from below deck?

Sarah stomps noisily into the bridge shuffling her feet in wet water logged boots. Noah shifts mental gears. "Great job Sarah - getting rid of that pesky whale saved us from a potentially life threatening event. I am also impressed with your comforting efforts in reassuring our jittery passengers on what will be their first night at sea."

Sarah shrugs off the veiled complements and confronts Noah with a question. "Why didn't Gold Almighty also doom all the sea critters? Some of them are pretty naughty, mean and nasty, like humans? Orcas are hardly your friendly next-door neighbors, unless you are a rock. Yes, I suppose it is difficult to drown fish, but God could have devised some other diabolical technique, like turning water to gas and putting a match to it. That would certainly fit His well documented former ka-boom life style."

"Sarah, my dear, remember we are not God or Goddess, and thus do not think like them. If God had wanted a gigantic fire ball fish fry to roast everyone in the sea that is of course what He would have done. But look how happily this drowning scheme is working out for us. We are the chosen lucky ones – at least this time. But perhaps if things should again get morally sticky, He might just take your suggestion to have a monstrous fish roast. Again, let me thank you for freeing the misbehaving whale." Replies Noah, who was always uncomfortable discussing issues of mass destruction and the like. "We must ark on – and on."

The ark bobbles unsteadily into its first night at sea. Fear and uncertainty permeates what is left of the land based animal kingdom. The animal pairs are skeptical of their future prearranged relationships. Since they had nothing to do with picking their upcoming mates, they are concerned about what effect this will have on established natural selection techniques. Incest in the animal kingdom had not been thoroughly researched, but they all had queasy feelings about interfering with nature's good intentions. The female baboon is eyeing her assigned mate and wondering if he could possibly be her brother. She loudly blurts out. "Yuck."

Noah is not concerned with family relationship issues, but is keenly aware of the ark's structural defects, including relentless leaks. Sarah is busily preparing for ark-board sit down meals, group entertainment, family counseling and sanitation. Busy, busy.

As if to say fare-thee-well, the sky is lit by a garish flash of golden lightening followed by deep rolling roars of thunder muffling into oblivion. Then silence, except for incessant wavelets slapping against the ark's wooden hull and the soft murmuring of frightened animals seeking to fall asleep with restless thoughts. Nightmares are rampant.

Noah is now officially a first time arker-boater. The ark is fully afloat with an amateur crew, a cabin full of stunned animals and a very dark night is settling in. The weather is unstable, The God and Goddess are nowhere in sight, but a conniving mean ass falcon is lurking somewhere in the ark's shadows. Noah is concentrating on brewing beer from rutabagas.

As Noah evaluates what is going on about him he thinks quietly to himself. "Wow - this arking life is the greatest!" A sentiment repeated by every sailor ever since.

CHAPTER 7

A SURPRISE VISITOR

The first night afloat passes surprisingly uneventful. The ark's rolling motion had a somnambulant effect on everyone. Getting on board and waiting for the rain water to rise had been an exhausting experience, the memories of which gratefully faded during the night. The uncertainty of their futures added a sense of adventure and so everyone slept like new babies, hoping tomorrow would bring clearness of purpose and joy to this cruising experience.

Midmorning and Noah continues mulling over the rudder problem when suddenly Falc appears on the bridge. Noah had not seen him since he told him to go get lost. Falc looks Noah straight in his one remaining eye, gives him a wink and darts off into the clouds. Why did she do that? Where is she going? just when I was beginning to maybe accept her visual talents and tolerate her on the bridge. Wonders Noah.

As if reading Noah's thoughts Falc quickly returns and tells Noah his plan. "Sorry for taking off without a comment, but I had to make sure my idea will work and no one but us two know about it. There is no one listening, just you and me, so here goes. We will make it appear to Sarah that I suddenly flew in from nowhere, like now. I then deliver a prepared presentation she absolutely can't resist. I am convinced that she will accept this cockamamie story. OK Captain, are you good to play along with the charade? Great!"

Without waiting for an answer Falc is again gone.

"What's up, dear Captain-Oh-My-Captain, I sincerely do wish to thank you for your complementary comments yesterday. You are not one to lavish praise on anyone, let alone me, your ever lovin', so what is really up?" asks the Captain's wily wife, Sarah.

Noah's palms are getting moist as he scrounges around in the bridge pretending to look for something. She must know about Falc, but how? A strange stillness prevails on the bridge as Noah continues his aimless search.

Sure enough, after a few minutes a dark bird appears far away in the sky and it is rapidly getting bigger. It comes swooping in and gracefully lands on Noah's shoulder, sitting regally next to his black eye patch covering the missing eyeball. Here is Mustafa's cunning falcon coming to play a critical role that she hopes will save her life.

Act One. With false indignation in his voice Captain Noah shouts: "Get off my shoulder you mean flea riddled falcon. I am still very angry with you for extracting my portside eye. Furthermore, God said we should only have one pair of falcons on this ark, which we already have. So vamoose and make it quick." Noah looks to Sarah hoping she will accept this amateur skit.

Act Two. The falcon speaks in a loud, firm, squeaky but demanding voice. "Look ole buddy Noe. I will call you Noe, and if you want to keep your other eyeball functioning normally, you better listen up. I intend, though I wish it wasn't necessary, to stay on this ark, of mostly fools until we land – somewhere. At that time, I will happily leave. But for now, I will be your first mate. Do we understand each other, Captain? Wink, wink."

Act three. "I am sure Falc, may I call you Falc, that we can work out an amicable arrangement for the rest of the journey. However as you know, my wife Sarah standing in front of us, sees her position as being first mate – so that issue will have to be resolved. But hey, you and I know who the real arkers are. You can take the helm at night since you have two good eyes and I will steer during the daytime with my one remaining eye. So, for now Falc, you are the ark's part time night-time first mate."

"Let's have a beer to toast this newly established leadership relation." Noah's thoughts are to get this amateur masterpiece theater over before Sarah catches on. "You falcons do drink beer in critical times, don't you?" Adding a touch of incredulity to a melodrama that is about to come unraveled, but for the moment Noah desperately hopes to distract Sarah.

Sarah, who had earlier been in the aft end of the ark busily shooing away whales, when Noah and the Falcon cooked up this skit, cannot believe what she is now seeing and hearing. But, she realizes the need for caution or her vision might also become impaired, or even extinct if this nitwit falcon should again behave as she had to Noah during the night of amateur sex identification process. But is this falcon really a female?

Act Four. Enter Sarah center stage. "Whoa - stop right now; I cannot believe what is going on here. Noah, just who is that ugly mouthy beast, who a second ago came flitting in unannounced and promptly plops himself on your shoulder next to your empty eye ball socket and brags about being your first mate? Something about this unkempt raptor reminds me of your description of Mustafa's nasty falcon, who, by the way, should by now be securely drowned."

Falc, completely ignoring Sarah's caustic comments continues to try and derail her well-founded suspicions: "Captain, you surely don't think I drink beer - do you?" I come from high bred bird families. His deflecting attempt at subterfuge, though weak was effective. I will toast to you – The Captain Noah. And of course skoal to you too Sarah, my first mate colleague. We will be a winning team." Pretty gutsy falcon.

Noah, now sensing the drift of his newly adopted first mate falcon: "No Falc, we have only beer for toasting, Of course we would all prefer Chivas. But let us now in good spirits focus on the inevitable joyful time we will spend arking together; it really looks like you, Sarah and

I, and our guests are in for a great, thrill a minute, seafaring cruise, regardless of drinks. Ha-ha." Captain Noah has at this moment become the trend setter for all future yachters; always keep plenty of beer on board for sticky situations.

In unison the two start making up and singing naughty sailor chants. Sarah is aghast, incapable of comprehensive speech, thinking this nautical lifestyle is driving everyone crazy, it must be that the constant wave action is short circuiting neurons.

Act five. "Sarah, my truly beloved, may I now formally introduce you to my dear friend Falc. True, he was solely responsible for my losing an eye when I tried to check out his rear feathers. Remember when I came home bleeding and you ever so lovingly patched me up?" Well, sure enough, Falc, overcome with remorse has for months been tirelessly looking for me, wanting to apologize and clear up our little unfortunate misunderstanding and subsequent brouhaha. What do you know, he found me, out here in the middle of this restless stormy sea during a dark night. He has profusely apologized and we are becoming good ole arking buddies.

Furthermore as you heard him say, he will take the helm at night so you and I can enjoy our lovey-dovey sleepy time. Isn't that just ducky? Sarah, you and I are the luckiest people in the world, not to mention the last two human adults left alive." Noah hopes against hope that this line of baloney will wash with Sarah.

A prolonged period of silence follows when everyone is busily positioning their replies and waiting for Sarah to assess this development. These are the tense moments that everyone dreads because everyone knows it always turns out badly, especially for the one brash enough to speak first.

The finale. "You know what ole buddy Noe? I will bet you that your long lost bosom fleabag Falc is a male; I know that without even touching any of his tender fluffy rear feathers. You were so out of it the night you conducted your birdie research you haven't a clue as to his gender. But I can tell from his overly bravado behavior he is definitely what you numbskulls call a stupid alpha male." Smirks the incredulous Sarah.

"Sarah you are right on both counts, I am a majestic male falcon and, you damn well better not touch my 'fluffy' rear feathers, if you know what I mean. Although a black patch over one of your bleary eyes might improve your general appearance; like it did for your wasted husband Noah. Do we understand each other?" Quote the falcon.

"Sure, sure, Falc. I won't touch your aft and you keep your talons on the helm at night. It's a deal. And I remain the ark's first day time mate!" Quote the Sarah.

The brief on board skit over command is over with no applause or encores, just an uneasy acceptance of what are the facts. From here on the falcon, now officially named Falc, will be recognized as a male and night time first mate. Finally - Falc graciously accepts a beer and draws a big sigh – for now his life is spared and he is arking in first class.

The master negotiator Noah has done it again. Noah's Ark remains a vessel of uneasy tranquility. It is now time for the first gala "at sea" meal function. Until now the animals survived poorly due to mal de mer, general malaise, and even depression. Food had not yet been a major issue. But now that the ark is fully afloat, with the cruise management team in place it is time to establish a routine beginning with meals.

Sarah has called for the attention of all the animals and announces in a booming commanding voice heard throughout the ark that there will be two seating's for dinner, and the first seating is about to commence. It will be all the large meat eating animals. Sarah believes getting these big bully passengers fed first makes sense.

Next comes Sarah's tricky "Blue Plate Special of the Day" announcement. Sarah has a loud voice, but it is quivering as she continues. "I have a very special surprise for all you meat eaters. You are now about to abandon your former bad saturated fat laden carnivore red meat diets and becoming healthy happy cholesterol and triglyceride lowered vegetarians. You will live much longer, enjoy a fuller life and have fewer aches and pains in the morning. Your arteries and the rest of your plumbing will flow fast and clear for an indefinitely long time. What a deal, right?"

"What in hell?" Roar the tigers, panthers and lions in unison. The two hyenas are busy choking and can't make any sound all. The birds of prey are wildly beating their wings together make a sound like "no way, no way, no way."

Sarah sensing some genuine unhappiness with this healthy diet decides to feed the two grumpy lions first to immediately defuse the tense situation in the dining room. Hopefully the tigers and other carnivores will follow their lead. She places a beautifully laid out plate of dry hay and sliced rutabagas in the lion's cage. The lion's collective four eyes each get bigger than the plate containing the hay and sliced rutabaga. They are totally dumb founded that some human being, i.e. Sarah, is so out of touch with the wild animal kingdom that she would attempt such a stupid thing. The two lions agree, "It is little wonder God and humans conjured up this nutty idea of drowning our relatives – they are alike with malfunctioning brains. Evolution skipped over them. Let's charge."

The two disbelieving tigers react differently, they sit motionless and silently for a few seconds as if in a stupor and then begin a mournful whimper while crying profusely on each other's shoulder. In a dirge like sound they loudly sob while chanting. "Hay and rutabagas, hay and rutabagas, go team go, go team go – over and over for five minutes without interruption. Their mental health is declining precipitously.

Then the chant suddenly stopped with; "Why, oh why, did you and God not let us drown like all the other bad lions and tigers; we are all accustomed to daily homicide, indeed that is how we survive, eh? What kind of unintended 'goodness' did we do to deserve these abusive hay and rutabaga menus? Please, dear Sarah, can't we at least share one of the lousy squeaky rodents? Alas, we are doomed."

Falc, a connoisseur mouse eater himself sizes up the explosive diet modification situation in a flash and realizes something must be done immediately or the lions and tigers will start eating any available red meat near them since they are now over their sea sickness and indeed very hungry. He hops over to the lion's cage and in detail lays out the nourishment situation and politely asks if they, like himself and Captain Noah, would be content with beer instead of hay and rutabagas. Their reaction is immediate; they smile and agree to be good little purring lions if they can have beer instead of hay and rutabagas. Again they look each other in the eye, wink and concur that a sailor's life may just be OK after all. And since their HDL and LDL levels will be dropping into normal range they are indeed content. The tigers quickly follow suit as do the hyenas.

Problem solved. Noah feels real smug about having Falc as a pretending half time first mate. He just solved a major confrontational issue. But of course giving beer to all the meat eating animals puts a strain on Noah's beer supply. So that night, he and Falc get together on the bridge and begin concocting a solution to their rapidly dwindling beer cache and the possible long indeterminate voyage ahead. For the moment the meat eaters are satisfied with beer but when it runs out we will need both an effective detox program and a substitute menu, ponders Captain Noah.

Sarah, who was certainly never personally a lush, also has some reservations. She worries that if these beer drinking raw meat eating carnivores find that beer also significantly increases their libido, then the projected repopulation strategies would need lots of adjustments upsetting the ark's ELS (estimated landing schedule), which continues to remain unknown?

Falc, being far more creative than Noah and Sarah, questions whether or not you can even ferment enough hay mixed with rotten rutabagas to make beer. Captain Noe and Falc continue their fermenting discussion late into the evening drinking, their now in short supply, beer while simultaneously performing celestial navigation consisting of looking at the ever slowly moving moon and unmoving stars.

They agree, tomorrow we must find a way to start an ark brewery. This was another first for boater Noah, designing a functioning brewery from its galley's pots and pans. Bigger question, will Sarah give up her pots and other cooking utensils to help make brewing a reality? So far, cute as inebriate animal behavior appears on the surface, Sarah remains unenthused and skeptical about semi drunken meat eaters lolling all over the ark purring and laughing their heads off. But interestingly enough, Sarah too, has quietly also developed a petite taste for beer so she realizes a shortage could be problematic, even for her.

For yet another time Captain Noah and Falc are faced with sweet talking Sarah; this time about the possibility of using her cooking hardware for brewing. "Dear sweet Sarah", coos Noe. "As we know you are the most dedicated person with the heavy responsibility of nurturing and counseling our varied passengers. Falc and I continually marvel at the generous manner in which you are tirelessly carrying out these challenging chores, always with compassion and never complaining. All the animals look sooo healthy and radiate inner peace and contentment. You are an absolute angel. What would this cruise be without you?"

"Cut to the quick Noe, this unusual flowery talk of yours is most unbecoming and is undoubtedly a not so subtle way of asking for something that you know I won't allow. This crap about me nurturing passengers to a high level of healthiness and spirituality has, thanks to your brain dead buddy falcon, now degenerated the ark's load of former meat eaters to a leaky bucket full of drunks, you two included. So just what is it you two sops want?" Responds a tired but savvy Sarah.

"Sarah sweetie, let me remind you, watching one's unbridled tongue will help preserve one's eyeballs. Civil language is a distinguishing quality first mates on long cruises should aspire to demonstrate at all times." Chirps Falc, while sharpening talons with his beak.

"You know what Falc, if you would listen more, and talk less, you might become a much smarter – as well as nicer – big birdie. This bit of sage advice also goes for our loony Captain and my husband." Quips Sarah.

Noah again comes to the rescue by deflecting the sarcastic conversational drift. "Well, my darling Sarah, as you can see all of us meat eaters are thoroughly enjoying sloshing through this directionless cruise. Just notice how our formerly voracious, tigers, vultures and boa constrictors are lovingly hanging all over each other whispering sweet nothings. Aren't they are just too cute for words? Thanks to a cooperative crew we all now enjoy unprecedented harmony and tranquility, some would call it nirvana." Captain Noah pauses to let his eloquent comments sink in.

"Even the rattlesnakes are enjoying this beer diet, notice they haven't rattled their rattlers since they took up drinking; they just lie there quietly as wooden sticks. Even stepping on them does not raise a rattle. No pun intended. The raptors have all taken to sleeping on their backs during both days and nights, with only an occasional loud impolite burp and minor bothersome snoring." Noah continues, trying to assuage and pussy foot the virtues of a fermented liquid health diet for the ark's animals when Sarah has had enough and sharply cuts in.

"Noah you, a former desert nomad bum, are establishing a very bad cruise tradition by suggesting that the only good cruise is a drunken cruise. But, I must admit it works, even I am taking a nip now and then. We have not had one squabble from you meat eating critters since we took up drinking beer. At times I do worry about long term effects on our bladders, livers and kidneys. Even you dear Noah, have been a real delight, exuding gentle smiles and a conviviality that I had never seen in you before. Thank you my sweetie Captain." Coos

Sarah, thinking to herself, I can dish out arking malarkey as well as my bridge mates.

Falc has had about enough of this drivel; there is a problem to be solved. "Hey you two, we have an emerging emergency that will put a quick and final end to this happy sea going life for all of us. Case in point - we are rapidly running out of beer. So what is your answer Sarah, can we use your pots and pans to jury rig a still or will the lions eat us? A simple yes or no will suffice. I got your message about talking too much."

"You must think I am crazy Falc, of course you cannot use my pots and pans, and furthermore you are a very bad influence on my dear sweet Noah," Rebuffs Sarah, who hates to be manipulated especially by a bird with equal rank.

"Oh, oh", respond Noah and the falcon in unison.

Noah again takes the high ground. "Look here Sarah, love of my life, we are rapidly approaching a true life threatening cruise crisis, and if we run out of beer the meat eaters on this cruise will be back on their regular steak and hamburger diet. And don't forget they might even take a fancy to your well endowed tush. We have got to keep making more beer and that means you sharing your pots and pans for the good of the masses. If we can brew eight hours a day we should be able to keep up with our voracious carnivore appetites as well as meeting our personal needs for peace, tranquility and happiness – not to mention staying alive."

"Oh, dear God, oops, by the way where is He, haven't seen Him since we cast off? OK, OK, I demure, better you make beer than the lions take a fancy to my cute hinny. I was just being stubborn. You may use my pots and pans, but rest assured, I am not at all happy about it, you understand." Replies Sarah as she struts out of the bridge down into the reeking passenger compartments of pens, sties and cages, but inwardly happy and hoping that the ark-made brewery will be successful.

"Whoopee" yell Noe and Falc as they see their future brighten.

"No No Captain, it is not whoopee time yet. Hang in there." Adds Falc. "But a-brewing we will go, ho, ho." Falc continues as he rushes into the galley selecting implements essential for their on-board brewery.

Noah finally nods off while Falc arks bravely into the dark night supposedly guided by the stars above. The fact that the ark isn't moving much for lack of a propulsion system, and it is so overcast no stars are visible, makes it easy for Falc to pretend keeping on course while proclaiming; "I am headed straight toward the North Star so you can rest easy Captain, at least until the fog sets in."

The cruise is going along as well as can be expected, a continuous supply of rutabaga-hay beer has tamed all the carnivores, which beer still does for sailors to this very day. The birds are enjoying pecking at the rotting wormy pre-brewed rutabagas, but occasionally will take a sip of the lager, which makes them chirp with a un-bird like bubbly hiccupy sound. Their own recycled deposits turn out to be a fantastic yeast substitute. The ark's environment is now definitely in balance and sustainable. Green peace fans would be proud.

Captain Noah was an astute observer, like all good sailors. The days at sea provided him with opportunities to discover cause and effect relations in the firmament. Whenever there were changes in the ripples or surface waves on the sea about him he noticed that the weather would often change shortly thereafter. Big fluffy clouds were not only beautiful but also predicted good sailing; while darker wispy cloud formations often indicated it was time to batten down the ark's hatches, making for a terrible stench below deck. After watching rain storms at various times followed by sunshine he cleverly coined an adage.

> Rainbow at night, arkers delight.
> Rainbow in the morning, arkers take warning.

Sarah discovered that when the ocean air was breezy and clear, she and the animals felt great, but when a storm was approaching everyone was grumpy. They referred to these emotional mood swings as highs and lows. Rutabaga beer was always the mood leveler.

By now Noah is getting truly bored with this monotonous sea life and weather forecasting. Noah's psyche does not adapt well to a state of perpetual serenity. He is an active sort. Furthermore the bright hot sun makes the air humid and heavy which in turn means frequent thunderstorms accompanied by flashes of lightning. Though these squalls provide a bit of relief, Noah is suspicious that they are caught in some kind of water warp, i.e. the sun heats the water, which rises, and then cools and falls back on them. The cycles are repeated endlessly and Noah can now flawlessly predict them. He calls it: Noah's Oceanographic Atmosphere Almanac, NOAA for short.

Captain Noah has not had a visit, or any sign from God since they first began to float; and is naturally becoming apprehensive that the ark will never again land solidly on terra firma. Maybe, just maybe, God forgot about them and they are doomed on an eternal zoo cruise to nowhere.

"Hey there Falc." orders Noah, "As the Captain of this here ark, it is my duty to send out a scout to see what lies ahead. What I want you to do is sober up for a day or two and make a reconnaissance mission flight to see if there is anything other than water as far as you can fly and see with your blood shot eyes."

"Aye, aye Cap" responds the semi snoozing falcon. "At least I have two eyes, but I have a better idea. Why don't we tether one of the long necked giraffes on top of the bridge and let him be our lookout feller, eh? The giraffe would enjoy some fresh air and might gain a bit of self esteem in knowing he is on God lookout duty. Everyone's ego is boosted by a feeling of worth. Right Captain?"

"No Falc. I will not endanger a giraffe by having him precariously perched on top of the ark, ego enhancing or not. He would be a living lightning rod, possibly leading to a fiery demise for us all. Not to mention how ridiculous it would make our vessel appear, should anyone see us. It is your flight assignment so get on with it. But your giraffe idea is not without merit, except for the negative curb side appearance." Commands Captain Noah.

"OK, Boss. I'll take to the wild blue yonder as ordered."

Following a couple of days of drying out, Falc wobbly takes off from the ark, but just barely as his out of practice aching wings occasionally slap the water's surface. As all pilots know you must have confidence in your ability to fly or you won't fly. Initially Falc is psychologically unsure of himself since he had not flown for a long time and had also been pretty heavily into the sauce, a very bad combination for aviators. Finally, Falc regains the hang of flying, his spirits are rekindled and he majestically rises and soars far and wide over the bounding main.

After flying and diving for several hours Falc triumphantly returns and sadly reports, "Nothing but water as far as my keen eyes can see. Get me a beer Cap, fast." This bravado behavior is typical of animals (including people) that fly, they simply have fun flying, gleefully return, having accomplished nothing and demand a beer.

"Yes sir" responds Captain Noah. "Hey wait a minute Falc; you don't give orders for the Captain to bring you beer. But, I will overlook your insubordination this one time even though you did not find any land, eh? That is truly worrisome."

Has the Almighty abandoned the ark and His now not so merry crew? Wonders Noah. How long can we keep this pace going without a sign of hope of any kind?

Restless nights ensue with frequent flashbacks to earlier discussions with God.

CHAPTER 8

TENSE MOMENTS

Days and nights blur passing fitfully and slowly. Many of the animals are in stage four depression, some have lost their ability to communicate politely with each other. They sit, stare and constantly nitpick. This is a troublesome development for the ark's ultimate repopulation mission. Attitudes must be improved or whoopee is in jeopardy.

Late one afternoon a ridiculous melee began when the two banshees, whose language is very different from all the other animal pairs, began a petty dust up. First one banshee began to pout, and then the other one became first remote and finally hostile. Their behavior degenerated to the point where they meanly nipped at each other instead of sharing their differences by necking and yodeling sweet nothings, like lovers should. This egocentric behavior would certainly not be conducive for any future growth in the banshee population. The inane banshee lover's spat continued for over a week, all the while infecting other animal pairs as well. It was like someone loudly breaking wind in an un-air-conditioned concert hall when no one is playing. Everybody got the message. The ark was rapidly becoming a seething caldron of unsociability, an unstable condition Captain Noah rated orange.

Sarah realizes some ark cruisers may be developing the notoriously well known deadly traumatic mental health cabin fever syndrome (CFS) often followed by violent outbursts. With limited on board psychological resources available to treat these problems the possibility of Noah's ark becoming an out of control mental institution loomed.

Testing ensued. Sarah's Ink blot test results only indicated they were running short on ink. The ark's long range survival purpose is now in jeopardy simply due to poor communications between animal pairs. Noah, the ultimate typical alpha male shrugged it off, saying this phenomena was not life threatening and - just like when he and Sarah had differences – no big deal – she would get over it by morning, Rorschach test or no.

Major contributing factors to these potentially volatile interpersonal social disruptions were that many land animals, especially former desert dwellers, were not accustomed to long sea journeys with pre-assigned mates. But more worrisome for morality's sake, they were not naturally monogamous. This was not a Club Med, or was it? In Noah's ark case, couples had been carefully selected to survive (the ultimate survivor game), and to repopulate, but unfortunately had not been selected on the bases of personality profiles. And if these lover spats did catch on among the majority of Noah's ark cruising couples, God would surely have a reason to be upset – again.

It fell to caregiver Sarah to become the master pre-nuptial counselor. Her challenge was to establish among these woe-begotten land animals a sense of respect, decency, understanding, caring, and a life fulfilling future where all animal dreams come true; as is every psychiatrist's professional sworn oath and commitment. Sarah did pioneer the animal mental health field while adrift on Noah's ark filled with lonely animals whose ids, egos and libidos where now confused. Sarah was definitely opposed to any mood enhancing drugs, except - with reservation – home made beer.

Captain Noah was reluctantly becoming deeply concerned about a Godly promised landfall that now seemed more elusive by each passing day. He decides to let some other flying creatures out of their cages and make sorties to see if they can find land. Falc is rankled;

he feels Noah may be losing confidence in him. All the fliers, except one, return without sighting any land.

A day later as Noah and Falc are quietly sitting in the bridge, one of the tiny released hummingbirds, who had earlier become lost from the flock returns, whips in, stops and hovers six inches in front of Falc's beak staring him straight in the eyes.

"What have we here?" inquires Falc. "How in the world can you fly, suddenly stop and finally hover in front of my beak like you are now doing? You are weird." Falc takes a swipe at the hummingbird with one wing, but wildly misses him and embarrassingly topples over on his left side. The hummingbird grins and zip - he is again momentarily gone. Falc is frustrated; he has never known a bird like this. Noah is smiling to himself.

The prideful falcon, Falc, does not like to be dumb founded and teased.

The clever little humming bird is now thinking that he may just be able stay out of his stinking cage below by entertaining the crew on the bridge as a bird ark jester. So he does a few more wild aerobatics that really captures their attention. This colorful little critter's seemingly random flitting about is most entertaining.

"Hey Cap, how does that hummer do those maneuvers? His antics are really not bird like at all. The cute little stinker does impress me. Let us keep him up here as the ark bridge entertainer, eh?"

Noah. "I surely don't know Falc, but if you would be nice to him he might share his aerodynamic secrets with you. He and his whoopee mate-to-be have been in their cage below deck this entire time and I am sure he is simply exuberant for having been given his freedom, if only temporary. Be nice to him."

"OK, I will do my best, Captain. Hey there sweet little Hummy, come over here – pretty please." Fakes Falc.

The agile Hummy again whizzes in, stops a few inches from Falc's beak and winks. Falc is furious, but retains his composure. "Hey, tell me little red green breasted Hummy, how in the world did you learned to stop in the air and then hover in place like you do? I surely wish you would teach me how, would you, pretty pleeeese?"

"Of course, it would be my pleasure to teach you Falc, but you have to follow my instructions explicitly. First, you relax your wings in their sockets by letting them droop. Then you whirl them around real fast. You falcons soar by keeping your wings relatively rigid and letting the wind carry you aloft. That is known as the lazy bird approach to flying. We hummingbirds have to work at it by spinning our wings – really fast. You must know our heart's beat hundreds of times a minute while you falcon's hearts are lucky to go ka-plunk twice a week."

"Here we go pal, slowly at first, follow me: Step 1, loosen your wings, and let them hang limp. Good work, big birdie. Now for Step 2, begin whirling them around as fast as you can. Got it? I will back up a bit to get a better visual perspective." Hummy can hardly keep a straight bird face in telling Falc what he has to do.

Falc lets his wings sag and then tries to spin them as instructed. The results were hilarious to everyone but Falc. As he wildly tries spinning his wings he falls off balance and topples to the bridge deck in a heap, loudly uttering bad bird words.

Hummy had to turn his face allowing his big grin to pass. Cap Noah is openly beside himself with raucous laughter. Falc is painfully struggling on the deck trying to right himself, while continuing to sputter vile invectives at Hummy. "I'll get you!"

Mischievously Hummy remarks, "That was an excellent beginning, at least for you – a puffed up falcon. You just need a bit more diligent practice and you will be as graceful as I." Hummy darts off doing a couple of barrel rolls before he too falls into laughter while spinning downwards toward the ark.

Captain Noah mercifully picks up his ego bruised First Mate Falc and lays him gently on a deck chair. Falc is in excruciating pain, complaining bitterly and barely able to move his wings. More importantly his persona has been so severely challenged that he is determined to master Hummy's craft or else. Tonight when everyone is fast asleep I will work really hard on this, he thinks to himself.

This day ends and all is well on the ark, except for Falc, who is still writhing in pain, but eager to fly like a hummingbird. Hummy has decided to stay out of his cage and has quietly settled down for the night atop the bridge smugly content with his victory over a raptor. "He is dumb, but has the guts to try – got-ta give him that."

Still no sight of land, only flashes of lightening on the horizon. God seems to be gone.

Early the next morning Cap Noah comes to the bridge and finds Falc still in a pitiful heap under the wheel, his talons dutifully grasping onto the helm. Falc is totally exhausted and beginning to realize he will never attain the much admired hummingbird flight status. He is a beaten big bird and begins to sob loudly as Noah once again picks him up and cradles him to his breast; Falc's spirit is crushed along with his wing rotor joints. It will be weeks before Falc can again move his wings and then only with great discomfort. For now Falc's soaring escapades and looking for land are over. The ark will have to rely on others, less noble birds for sighting land. Falc is physically crippled and emotionally humiliated. A mighty falcon's psyche has been devastated by a tiny hummingbird. There is no avian justice.

During the next night, while Falc was practicing aerobatics in his dreams. Hummy quietly flew his perch and did not return in the morning. Falc and Noah slowly began realizing how much they missed the little guy's flying antics and sassy humor. "Why did he leave us?" They lament, "We didn't mean to hurt his fragile feelings, though he is a challenge, especially for us big birds." Moaned the aching Falc.

Falc continues. "I have a hunch that our sneaky little imp has indeed found land and will not share his findings with us. Remember how quiet he was when he returned from his recon mission? Boy, have we been taken. All I have left is two aching, mutilated wing joints and a very badly bruised raptor's self-image. That flash in the pan bird is living it up somewhere, I'll just bet he found land but kept his beak shut so we wouldn't follow?"

Stoically Captain Noah adds. "Yeah mates, that's life at sea."

CHAPTER 9

SAILING ON AND ON

Days on the ark's bridge continue to pass slowly, at times the crew looses hope they will ever find a shore. The relentless sloshing of waves softly lapping on the hull produces a sense of eerie monotony for Captain Noah and the bruised falcon. There was little for them to do except drink warm beer, wistfully banter about esoteric philosophies of life and take cat naps; pretty much in that order. That was life on the bridge.

For Sarah it was an entirely different world. Feeding the always hungry animals tasteless veggies was exhausting, but not nearly as taxing as keeping them happy, or at least keeping them from not killing each other. Sarah had learned from earlier experiences with depression that the best solution was to take preventative measures, and that meant keeping their minds occupied with joyful and meaningful activities. So as all good practitioners of the pseudo science of psychology, Sarah was constantly plagued by what to do to keep the animals entertained. The two donkeys had had it with everyone gleefully pinning false tails on their sore acupunctured behinds. They now booed instead of brayed.

Then one day Sarah, in a peak of frustration coupled with the cruising blahs, recklessly tosses a piece of hemp rope into the primate enclosure with a verbal expletive. The monkeys rolled in laughter at their new toy. At first they simply whipped it around each other, but then they began twisting and turning it until it looked like a monkey's clenched hand. Sarah thought it was cute, gave the monkeys extra rations and named their decorative creation the monkey fist. The gorillas just sat, glared and reflected on the fact that idiocy reigns.

"We must do more of these creative activities!" proclaimed Cap Noah. "We'll sell these knots in the souks and malls throughout the world once we hit land." Noah was like all sailors, looking to get rich – quick, with minimum effort and at someone else's expense.

Since the ark had a diverse complement of two by two animals, every pair naturally evolved many interesting on board activities. Knot tying had to stop because the monkeys almost inadvertently hung a defenseless rabbit that had mistakenly hopped into their cage. Captain Noah made an executive order that there will be no more near, nor out and out hangings, on board his ark. The directive extended to keel hauling and walking the plank.

Music was always a favorite activity, as it is today for everyone at sea. The best orchestral effort consisted of each animal making their own natural noises producing a wild cacophony that sounded much like rap singers doing yodeling style Wagner operas. Often, in order to get a complete range of in-depth sounds various natural gases were released by the animals adding a sound dimension to musical events never found in modern symphonic productions. Sound is based on vibrations that can come from a variety of sources. This is true.

Sarah concluded: The range of behavioral differences in animals at sea is exactly like it is for humans and furthermore you treat them the same way. She also began thinking that there may be a strong case for evolution – if so, how will this drowning theory improve anything? Noah's ark load of survivors will simply go on evolving in their own naughty nasty way as before. Unfortunately Sarah's daily mundane chores kept her mind focused, behavioral and philosophical theories would come later.

A new activity chart was posted every morning on one of the ark's bulkheads. It was the responsibility of each animal to read and then participate in their assigned event. On occasion this led to bruised feelings. Many of the timid cruisers felt they should not be asked to perform in a manner incompatible with their inner selves and belief systems.

Boa constrictors were assigned to loosen up at the bar by drinking beer while the hares and rats worked out on spinning treadmills. The two cats were cuddled by Sarah all day long (she just loved cats), while the dogs had a series of hydrants to visit on a prearranged scheduled. Bats were given an exception; they could flit about at night and stay quietly in their makeshift cave during the day.

And so their arking life passed, day after day. Sarah creatively managed to provide meaningful and life fulfilling activities for all the animals. She was a master and a totally successful human and animal resource manager who developed healthy behaviors except for the ark's Captain Noah and his flippant part time first mate. The two refused to exercise, follow good nutritional habits, read inspirational materials and think clean thoughts. Sarah tried valiantly to enrich their paltry intellectual and spiritual lives, but finally gave up on them and concentrated on the passengers below. "You can't win them all."

Nights at sea were devoted to heated cosmological discussions, about the meaning of life and who is in charge. Observing the infinite number of twinkling lights became the focus of what was God's master plan. Just how all this fit together with them bobbing relentlessly in an ark above the desert after everyone else drowned became a mental challenge. Every answer they conceived made no sense. "We seem to be missing something." quipped the sage Captain Noah.

Falc. "Yeah, right Captain, it is your lack of pattern recognition that plagues you humans; you just don't get it, do you? Let me explain; if you look carefully night after night, as we have, you will see certain clusters of light that seem to outline something. See that grouping over there; doesn't it look like a hunter with a belt who may be out stalking one of us animals? That bunch over there reminds me of a bull, another a lion, a bird like me, and to the left is the outline of a crab."

"You are so right, Falc." This was the first time that Sarah had really expressed her appreciation of Falc's comments and intellect. "You are really on to something. Why don't we each select a cluster and tell a story about it?" Sarah would have made a great primary teacher.

"Great idea, Sarah." raved the puffed up falcon, now feeling proud that both his visual acumen and cosmological insights were finally making him acceptable with the Captain's wife.

Great, here we go, thought Noah. "My wife and my part time night time first mate and former eye remover Falc, have finally bonded. It is true women do innately love birds. That is good, now perhaps a little more tranquility will develop on my bridge."

Falc, because of his incredible eyesight, later discerned that the star patterns also occurred with predicable regularities. They soon recognized there was a circular band of shapes that seemingly spun around one star. They flippantly named this belt of light figures the, "The Zoo" in honor of the arks passengers. This later became the zodiac.

The sky at night, big and bright, provided constant entertainment and soul searching. Every night as the winds and waves subsided a sense of awe and wonderment set in on the bridge. It was a time for all to meditate and fret about their future. Bad news, the ark was running low on rutabagas.

On the issue of who is really in charge of the universe they could not agree. Captain Noah was having itchy nagging feelings about his ole buddy God, who after all got him into this offshore life style but now is nowhere to be seen. Is he really the head tamale of the universe? But if he isn't, then Noah worries they have really been duped. Noah begins to worry that he, crew and passengers may become the first flying nomad Dutchmen in an ark on a desert sea.

Sarah too, has had some nagging reservations about the concept of heavenly sincerity – especially ever since the Goddess failed to show for the ark's launch due to hair problems. Come on, you can always plaster hair down with a dab of camel dung.

However, they agreed that dwelling and fixating on uncertainties in the universe provided no certainty at all, except for the fact that you can do it forever. Falc referred to this as the Cosmic Funny Fractal. Noah. "Please no more math Falc."

CHAPTER 10

ARRIVAL

A brilliant multicolored sunset is again rejuvenating the intrepid cruiser's souls as they regally sit on Noah's bridge drinking beer and philosophizing. Falc, whose wing rotor sockets, now almost healed, keeps coming back to how much he still misses Hummy and his flying antics. "I am really sorry I lost my temper when that twit showed me up on aerobatic flying, after all I am a falcon with the sharpest eyes in the desert."

"You are right Falc, Hummy sure knows how to maneuver and test your inflated self-image, ha-ha. Just try to be patient and learn from him, OK?" Always remember greatness often comes in tiny packages." teases Capt Noah.

"You humans really do not appreciate the intellectual nature of us birds. True, our brains are puny compared to total body weight, but we have learned how to use what we are given, no entitlements. You Homo sapiens with your large hunk of apparently inert grey stuff can at best walk and sort of swim, but never fly. How embarrassing this must be for you, right? responds the ever flippant Falc.

Sara and Noah ignore Falc's barb, but realize there is some validity to his comments. Indeed if there is evolution then humans seemingly were often left behind the door – maybe most of the time. They agreed that God's big Ka Boom was an enigma yet to be solved. "How, is one issue, but why is another." This they could all agree on.

As they sit peering into a gorgeous colorful western sunset a small vibrating dot seems to be slowly fluttering across the waves as it approaches the ark. It flies in a most erratic pattern. "Cap, do you see a little wiggly spot drifting just above the water on the starboard side?" asks Falc.

"Yes indeed Falc," Replies Noah as he squints towards the strange shimmering object nearing the ark, trying to identify the apparent intruder. "Could it finally be a sign from God?"

Then it happens in a flash. Hummy comes screaming in at breakneck speed and does a double loop four inches from Falc's beak. Falc recoils expecting to be hit straight on. Noah exhibits a big grin as he recognizes the interloper. Sarah wonders what now?

Hummy has returned.

Falc is initially not moved, Sarah had almost forgotten the nervous hummingbird. However all concur that this is a fantastic event. They laugh and chirp that their bridge mate has come back to them. "OK, Hummy, come aboard and rejoin our crew." Yells Captain Noah.

Falc quickly recovers emotionally and wants to know where in this wide wet world Hummy has been for the last few weeks. "We really missed you squirt and I am so sorry for the mean nasty things I said about your flying prowess. Gosh, it really is good to have you back among us." Falc, showing his affection, gently taps Hummy with his huge wing.

"Oh, not to worry mates, I decided we all needed a break from each other. I have flown far and wide, seen things you won't believe and had a heck of a great time. I now know exactly where we must go. Just keep heading west. " Exclaims the jubilant vivacious hummingbird. "Thanks for the touch Falc."

Hummy continues. "My aerial adventures took me to vistas beyond belief. This one place I spotted nicknamed 'Sin City' is full of voluptuous and scantily clad ladies. This I assumed is due to the high desert temperatures. Their significant others incessantly throw money and cubes with dots on them – and you'll never believe this – they seldom get any money back for their efforts. The entire concept is based on mathematics that accurately guarantees ultimate failure. To top it off everyone knows this but they love doing it anyway. Talk about dumb. Their motto; be a happy looser. Play again and be happier losing even more. Loosing has become an advanced life style for these strange humans living in their parched desert. It even pays their taxes. I tell you truly it is magical. I also discovered that many of these human types become politicians based solely on multiple failures and smooth talk - like mostly lies. This mind boggling merry-go-round is constantly evolving and led by whom else – lawyers."

Cap Noe ignores Falc's caustic remarks but remains curious. "Tell me Hummy, why isn't Sin City under water? Why didn't God's deluge engulf their brazen behinds?"

"Captain as always you put your finger on a hot touchy spot. My avian calculations backed by keen observations indicate that the God and Goddess's shower did not produce anywhere near enough rainfall to cover certain high spots on the earth. As I flew over parts of the planet I saw many places clearly above the newly established sea level created by God and Goddess. My guess is God's arithmetic skills were somewhat marginal. Working with pi is not easy. I do so enjoy mathematics." Brags Hummy.

"Right on Hummy." Injects the blusterous Falc. "Higher order thinking skills, ha, ha, they all need more developmental math, don't you think?"

Dang, muses Captain Noah, how will I explain this Hummy mathematical revelation to God, once the existing water levels subside and if He ever shows up? It will be an embarrassment to compare God's obvious mathematical faux pas to the spot-on correctness of Hummy. But on the other hand, if many of these purported to be alive humans are currently having a blast at losing, there may be hope for the rest of us. With a bit of luck we may sail our decrepit ark right into this fun loving Sin City's quay. We are seemingly already God-less. I wonder where he went – and why? Probably due to pure embarrassment - lack of math skills will get you.

Noah is now muttering to Hummy. "All this attention to mathematics is more than a nuisance; perhaps we should ask you birds to teach us some fundamentals. We will call it bird brain math for people or, math for bird brain people, or more directly - chicken math for the masses."

Strange, thinks Noah to himself. If the universe was created by a loving God, with limited math skills, how is it there are infinite possibilities, some good, some not so good, arising out of His well intended creation? Is it perhaps true that the lack of math skills is the real reason for universal chaos? If creating the Garden of Eden was His primary purpose, how did we end up with hellish behavior requiring drowning as a solution? This enigma later became known as "The Drown Theory".

Noah muses. Seemingly drowning became the Q.E.D. of a decadent life that began with fig leafs, asps, bad apples and poor math scores. And now according to my clever feathered observant hummingbird crewmember Hummy, drowning apparently isn't working that swiftly either. If Hummy is correct that folks are still partying in Sin City, where being a loser is defined to be eternal happiness - we really do have a problem. I must retake Beginning Pre - Algebra to comprehend all this. Building this ark was easy compared to figuring out why to build one in the first place. Maybe this means that, "why" trumps "how". Hmmm?

Everyone on board the ark is jubilant since Hummy has ventured out and returned with welcome news that there is land and that some humans are enjoying gambling where the rising waters didn't rise high enough. The bedraggled ark animal cruisers also begin taking solace in the fact that if there are dumb rich folks somewhere, some of them might just take good care of their animals – oh, to be so lucky, to live among the ignorant rich who love pets. Fat chance thinks the hyenas. Today this feeble animal wish has become accepted as the political foundation for the modern Chicken House Trickledown Theory.

Sarah and Noah remain unsure of how to bring this fast breaking eye-witnessed news, espoused by their cavorting Hummy, to God and Goddess, should they ever return. These divine folks might get really upset and then what? A bigger shower?

Nevertheless hope springs eternal throughout the ark's beastly breasts. Cockatoos, parrots, turkeys, and related fowl kin, are naturally elated and begin incessant cackling, while the more conservative cows, who are less optimistic about their future, also begin mooing more softly, but inwardly leery of again becoming future prime and t-bone steak providers.

Hummy's news proclaiming he has seen lush green fields is nonetheless euphoric and contagious. Noah's ark of personally selected paired refugees had become a floating stinking simmering kettle of discontent, where knot tying contests caught on only with the apes and monkeys. The rest languished in despair. But a potential land-ho, even if dubious, is every arker/sailor's dream, and so it was on Noah's ark.

Hummy is heralded as the ark's absolute hero. Falc, crestfallen, but accepting the fact that he was not the first to sight land, is magnanimous and publicly congratulates Hummy. Every animal on the ark is chirping, hissing, growling, moaning or bellowing the happy news – there is land – our beloved Hummy saw it and brought back details. He can't be wrong.

Captain Noah remains skeptical and realizes he must send more aerial scouts to verify Hummy's as yet unsubstantiated land discovery claim. He decides to send more birds with short range flying capability; not the albatrosses and geese that might just take off never to return, fantasizing they are again on some kind of endless migration. Noah is also reconsidering Falc's earlier idea of tethering a giraffe on top of the bridge as a backup spotter plan. "Who is out there to ridicule this grotesque looking ark anyhow?"

Finally it happens, just as everyone is settling in for happy hour on the bridge, in fly several of the scouting birds, mainly terns and mud hens, excitedly supporting Hummy's claim; they too had spotted a verdant sweet smelling meadow. It was so beautifully bedecked with dark green grass, red, blue and yellow flowers blooming. "Can't we return immediately?" they pleaded. "We must go back tomorrow, please."

"Captain Noah." Triumphantly screams Hummy, who is now on a hero's roll. "It is the Nuevo Eden I told you about. I told you, I told you. Just incredible, we must land the ark and begin making whoopee with our mates. Whoopee, Whoopee!" That word whoopee, now becoming gospel, spreads like fire among the ark's passengers. Sarah is reminded that this word whoopee has at least two meanings.

Noah and Sarah, while greatly relieved about land fall, are worried what to do next. Troubling and disconnected random thoughts and visions race feverishly through their tired minds. Item of deep concern - a French Bastille type rebellion is a possibility with everyone reverting to former long forgotten behaviors, i.e. eating each other. God and Goddess seemingly did keep their word about land, but where are they now with follow-up instructions? Everyone is exhausted, it has been a long arduous voyage of going nowhere; cruising is not for the faint of heart. Raw meat eaters are sobering up with loud roars. The ark is running dangerously low on beer. Amateurish whoopee making is beginning in some cages. Every animal's mind is on overload, sensing unfathomable pleasures, long denied, and now so tantalizing close in new uncharted lands. Just like any modern cruise boat going ashore seeking new adventures.

"Hi Ho, we must go to the Promised Land. Hi Ho, Hi Ho." Former pouting behavior among the pairs of animals is passé as they now begin expressing renewed desires for each other. It is a grandiose love fest in the making.

Abruptly the ark is jarred to a complete stop. It has run aground. Animals and loose objects are flying all about, some overboard. Screaming and screeching, mooing and hissing, roaring and whimpering, together make a Woodstock like sound echoing across the still partially water logged desert. Simply overpowering.

"Oh dear God." Yells Captain Noah, "We are so close to the Promised Land, and yet there is no way that my big lazy drunken animals can swim the distance to the beckoning shore. Noah's woe begotten ark is firmly hung up on a desert sand dune while so near to the perceived nirvana. Alas, we are doomed. This grounding was how our voyage began and now it is ending the same way. Oh, the ultimate irony of it all." Noah is tempted to use bad words, but remains a true nautical gentleman, as his mother had taught him.

There is mass bedlam on the ark. Flying animals fly off convinced they can make it, while flightless animals are restlessly scurrying about snorting and often recklessly jumping overboard. Snakes and related slithering kin are guilt ridden and losing their collective grip on life, mindful of their ancestor's mistake in the Garden of Eden that has resulted in this frightful drowning venture. "Just wait and see; we will again be blamed for imparting knowledge." Hisses the poor cute little garden snake. Rodents who were looking forward to burrowing are emotionally crushed realizing they too can't swim or burrow the distance. Solid good for digging dirt is so close and yet so far. Meer cats are all on their haunches hoping to see something meaningful.

Exuberance and sadness reign simultaneously. For every happy animal there is a terrified animal. The ephemeral well-known mask of the theater is hopping and dancing about everywhere. Tragedy and comedy accurately describe Noah's ark at this moment.

Unceasingly the unstable ark continues rocking back and forth on the dune below. The carnivores, who have been sobering up, now desire to eat somebody – anybody, just so it is bloody and red. Captain Noah makes another split second decision. "Sarah, begin serving beer as though you were the Grande Dame beer maid at Munich's Oktoberfest." Sarah also realizing the looming crisis quickly does as ordered, but aware of their short supply.

Slowly an uneasy serenity settles in. However, the tranquility is short lived. The ark's heavies; hippos, rhinos, and elephants have all moved to the port side of the ark, causing the ark's rocking motion to increase to a point where capsizing is a real possibility. A capsized ark is not a pretty landing. Captain Noah had warned God of this problem as they were embarking - a long time ago.

Many are getting seasick and are for sure frustrated. What a mess. The stressed Noah is for the first time on the verge of panic, when suddenly the ark begins to again bob and move. Déjà vu. By leaving, the charged up departing animals have, in combination with a slowly rising tide, refloated the ark. The lightened vessel lumbers ever so slowly towards the beckoning shoreline and by early evening it is solidly anchored on a beautiful sandy beach within easy walking, crawling or slithering reach of land.

Almost everyone, except Sarah, Falc, Hummy and Captain Noah bolt for the beach leaving the ark a somber and lonely hulk stuck firmly in a sand bar. "What an ungrateful bunch of cruisers." explodes the completely exhausted, but greatly relieved Noah. "God should have drowned every one of them, and maybe us too." For those remaining on the ark this final climatic moment of landfall is anything but joyous or victorious.

Noah asks Sarah to get them a beer. Sarah, completely exhausted is furious. "Get your own beer." Noah, not in any mood for another marital spat gets beer for the four of them. They all sit pensively staring into space still wondering what their future holds. In the far distance the gay euphoric muffled sounds of whoopee can be heard.

Noah has a troublesome thought after his first sip. "Oh Dear God, it all begins anew."

Suddenly out of nowhere the God and Goddess quietly appear on Noah's bridge, beautifully dressed and groomed, gleaming and glowing with enthusiasm. "You folks really did it – wow - what a truly magnificent Godly accomplishment – you must be ever so proud of yourselves." Chuckle the two Deities who had of course masterminded this epic cruise.

'My, oh, my yes," Echoes the exuberant Goddess, who is sporting a proper coiffure, with immaculately manicured nails and dressed to the nines in bright blue and white nautical denim attire. She is carrying a tiny tinkling ship's bell that she continues to jingle which in turn jangles Noah's shattered nerves. "We must celebrate this victorious drowning occasion with a proper Dom Perione toast. Surely dear Sarah, you have a few bottles cooling in the fridge that we can break out to commemorate this momentous occasion. Right dear?"

Sarah who has seemingly been at sea forever, without the benefit of a beauty salon, looks like she has been filling Iowa silos with frozen corn cobs for several years. Her hair is kinky, disheveled and matted with assorted bird droppings. Her clothes are at best rags that lack being washed since the cruise began. The aroma surrounding poor Sarah would challenge any French perfume maker. She may appear San Francisco hippie chic, but definitely not heavenly chic.

An explosion erupts in Sarah's head. This is not a normal Tylenol solvable headache, but one brought on by months of stressful yachting with a host of sloshed carnivores and an ego maniac husband defending a wily falcon that had earlier scratched his eye out. No, No, this is a nuclear fusion headache seeking to blow a hole in the earth's upper atmosphere to be witnessed by other life forms in the Milky Way galaxy.

Often overly stressed females tend to have a religious experience in times of grave crises, i.e. it is God's will, and then they tend to hunker down. But at this moment these reactions do not apply to Sarah. Initially she goes catatonic and cannot speak or move, totally frozen in time and space. All Sarah's bodily motions cease, including her eye balls. Sarah is possessed by demons. Her staring eyes and foaming nostrils are like those of a mad dragon, spewing out acrid smoke and searing flames. Sarah's still restrained spirit is now determined to destroy everything in her way and the Goddess better look out.

Oblivious to Sarah's altered state of mind, happy guy Captain Noah requests Sarah to be a good host and please bring all of them a round of fresh rutabaga beer instead of champagne. "I don't believe our champagne is cool yet." Noah's intended calming comment instantly ignites Sarah's sensitive detonator igniting the explosive charge.

Sarah explodes. After all this time on the briny with a boatload of drunken sex starved animals, coupled with the demeaning attitude of Noah, Falc's chauvinism, Hummy's half baked philosophies and finally the Goddess's request for chilled champagne to help celebrate this hilarious cruising experience, is simply too, too much. After all, Sarah's previous life style as a former tent homemaker on the Ratatat desert had in no way properly prepared her for these kinds of life enhancing social encounters.

At first Sarah screams, then yells naughty words and finally impulsively bites the ear of a poor non-comp-us-mentis Holstein cow that happened to be strolling nonchalantly on the deck, completely aloof to the unfolding drama. Poor thing didn't even know the ark had grounded. The wounded cow immediately goes berserk from ear lobe pain and bovine embarrassment. At first she emits an enormous cloud of yellow sulfur laden wind, as all cows will do naturally when stressed. Then with a loud bellow she charges off the ark's aft end, her tail sticking straight up in the air as she readies to fire again. Luckily she lands safely on all four legs and races off to the shore to join her designated male companion who is now a frustrated restless bull wondering where his loving partner has gone. However, whoopee is now not on the cow's mind. During these last few seconds of fright and flight all her amorous emotions were drained. Being bitten by a human - how gross; and now buster bull wants to run off into the woods. If there ever was a holy cow moment – this was it.

Sarah's unshackled and flamboyant display of intense unhappiness with the Goddess's request for champagne, is if nothing else pitifully entertaining. But the outburst serves to quickly and effectively release all her pent up hostile feelings over a simple innocent request for some chilled bubbly. The mushroom cloud is now dissipating. Spectators to this event are aghast, speechless and drinking heavily for fear of what might happen next. The cow episode had been most unnerving.

Sarah's hysterical storm inexplicably subsides and she demurely does get and serve the tepid rutabaga beer with a flare, hoping the Goddess will take her for a stiff one later on, right after she has killed Noah. God, feeling obligated, takes a long slow sip of Sarah's beer, grimaces, swallows, turns pea green and runs to the edge of the ark to relieve himself. The Goddess naturally can't stand the hay and rutabaga beer either and reacts violently by spewing it out all over the bridge, greatly upsetting Captain Noah. Falc, becomes infuriated at their ungodly behavior, and realizing that his homey little bridge is stained with beer is about to extract an eye from the Goddess, but thinks better of it.

For sure, more aimless squabbling ensues. Everyone is finding something, however petty, to complain about, if it isn't the beer's body, it's the color or aroma. Noah finally reminds them that it was beer that kept the ark's passengers from devouring each other. As always, it is Noah who masterfully calms troubled psyches, but sadly realizes that his first successful ark landing is rapidly becoming a social disaster all over the issue of bad beer. Even today these conditions often prevail when a yacht returns safely to its port.

Goddess and Sarah, as females are inexplicably apt to do, quickly settle their petty differences and agree the ark should have brewed either a rich merlot or a light fruity Shiraz. Sarah softly comments; "Goddess, you know well that guys are incapable of thinking about drinking anything but warm homebrewed beer."

A new topic emerges that they can both relate to. The Goddess demurely asks Sarah whatever happened to the gaudy Gucci knock off tote bag that she had earlier given her as a bon-voyage present. In reality it was just a bag made from old camel hair. "Oh dear Goddess, thanks for noticing, it was the geezer male Billy goat that one night took a shine to me and I had to cold conk him with it in order to maintain my integrity. Even after I knocked him silly he managed to tear it apart. I finally threw it overboard hoping that he would follow, but alas he did not."

The Goddess was beginning to regret she had not taken the cruise. It sounded like fired up fun. "Perhaps next time God opens another water world I can join."

"Dear God – oops - we will just have to get shopping and find you a new one. Today's styles are so cool - you just can't be seen without one." chirps the Goddess. "By the way Sarah what kind of cuisine did you all have on the cruise?"

"Tee Hee." laughs an impish Sarah. "While one-eyed Noah and his grumpy Falc were scrounging my pots and pans to make their still, I managed to rescue a single skillet. And as luck would have it, the female turkey began laying eggs, one every other day. I would alternate frying it sunny side up or make a rutabaga omelet. The crew never caught on; to this day it remains the turkey and my secret. She was such a sweet thing."

"Oh, you little devil Sarah."

Throughout this female banter God wisely keeps his mouth shut but has some strong thoughts about His entire drowning venture that is slowly beginning to seem like another debacle. How can I go wrong so often? If I ever have any kids I will certainly get them started on arithmetic early on.

Goddess and Sarah decide to take off on a shopping spree. "After you mates finish your beers, how about tidying up the ark before we return? Remember, cleanliness is next to Godliness. I have another tip for all of you - singing happy sailing songs often helps when doing menial chores around a boat. Ta-Ta chums, may the swabs be with you." They giddily gush while disembarking the reeking ark for mall hopping.

Noah is taking stock of the ark's physical condition thinking, "It really did OK, in spite of the abuse. I am a good builder of arks and just maybe someday I will open up an ark-yard, preparing for the next deluge, or just to go fishing.

God, trying to bring some clear understanding to this His most recent episode in His universe's growth and development plan, cannot find much to be elated about. He is embarrassingly conscious of the unrestrained gleeful activity in the new found land but just what is this Sin City all about? By My faulty rainy miscalculations many apparently did not get soaked enough to drown. "Maybe I am taking My creator's job too seriously. Surely there must be more to life than math, bad beer and drowning. I still have high hopes for the life of arkers; I must not forget that thought." Muses God as He surveys the discordant scene unfolding around Him but appreciating the fact that He is standing on a magnificent ark isolated from the merriment of animal activity, including shopping. Sailors do indeed have the best lives.

Reflections by the author. At this point in my Noah revelation project a troubling pattern was emerging. God Almighty was truly between many dunes and wet spots, when He called for a devastating shower to rejuvenate his original start-up plan. He and his Missus had lovingly created and beautifully decorated a peaceful garden where all animals could freely romp about as long as they wore proper fig leaves and asked no metaphysical questions. But the minute their leafy britches fell off and they began asking questions, there were plenty of asps in The Garden to give wild ass answers that led them all far astray. God's soaker was clearly justified, but the desired results were now far from conclusive.

Almost immediately following this watery cleansing episode, many animals seemed to be reverting back to prior times, whooping, shopping and consuming mightily. The ladies had abandoned the guys on their stinky, almost derelict ark, for the malls. The birds were back to seemingly mindless chirping. Slewing and slaying were perhaps just around the corner as soon as populations grew a bit to sustain the activity. The stress levels on planet Earth's resources were again rising feverishly. Finally, to add to His woes God was also faced with the possibility of a host of upstart second string gods whose credentials were uncertified, but all were madly seeking to be the NOG (Number One God). It seemed that it might be Falc's Chaotic Chaos theory that was running rampantly through the universe, possibly concocted and nourished by rogue deities.

All these factors made God's future challenging, bleak and uncertain. At this point I was tempted to quit the NOAH project, but I could not. Extraterrestrial forces would not allow me. It was to become more intriguing and exciting. May we continue.

CHAPTER 11

FREEDOM & HUMOR

Fatigued and emotionally drained God, Captain Noah, Hummy and Falc, sit quietly on the bridge sipping their remaining rancid beer, wondering if this historic experience was really worth all the travails. "Hey, there mates, this is not what I had in mind when I signed up for this cruise." offers the melancholy Falc, who had failed to be the first to sight land.

"Wait just one minute Falc; you did not sign up, you simply imposed yourself because you didn't like the idea of drowning. Let us keep the record straight." Retorts Noah, who has tired of the falcon's snippy and self serving comments.

The four males; a God, a human and two birds are frustrated and are not even able to sustain any petty squabbles. All are mentally drained and almost motionless. Their future appears uncertain, unless they can come up with a scheme – which in general - males can. However, they have few attractive alternatives, actually only three. Go shopping with the ladies, drink more stale beer or go back to sea. God perks up. "You know what - we could do two of the three options, couldn't we?"

"That is ingenious God. No wonder you are God. I know exactly which two options we should do." Falc has suddenly and enthusiastically sensed what God has in mind and his spirits rise.

Hummy remains silent, but inwardly relishing thoughts about all the great things he had seen on his extended flights over Sin City. These places would be worth another in depth visit. "I might even take a go at the tables."

More beer is drunk; life is renewed as they all agree that Noah's beer is really not that bad once you get enough of it. Planning for the next voyage moves feverishly ahead by incorporating the knowledge and skills learned in their first momentous trendsetter journey. Bad times at sea are quickly forgotten while new and better experiences are anticipated. For sailors the future is always bright. You never have a half full sail.

Captain Noah gingerly brings up a poignant question to God. "We discovered during our cruise that this ark design of yours has some serious inadequacies – no offense you understand. A long voyage with a destiny in mind is not the same as endlessly bobbing up and down on a huge desert pond. Getting somewhere is something else. We need a source of propulsion and a method of control." The era of naval technology has formally arrived, here and now.

Noah is not only a smart arker, but also a smart sailor. Thinks God. Selecting Noah was a masterful decision and I must keep him on my roster for future Godly and/or un-Godly adventures. Good man!

"You hit the nail on the head Cap, and I have just the answer." Interjects the now fully re-energized Falc. "I will hold out one of my wings and you guys make a huge replica of it. We will then attach it upright on the ark. You all know how well I can soar; now we will use this same principle of wind flowing over an aerodynamic surface to propel our pregnant looking ark horizontally on the surface of the sea."

"Great idea, but won't it tip over?" Inquires the ever cautious Noah.

"Yes it will Cap – but if we attach a heavy weight, that we will call a keel, for lack of a better name, to the ark's bottom it will not tip as easily. responds Falc. "God - why in the world did you not think of this?"

"Hey Falc, get off my back, you know I admire math but was just too busy to do the homework. However, I concur that your idea is truly a nifty patentable concept that I should have thought of, but don't rub it in, OK?" Retorts God, who is obviously peeved by Falc's constant irreverent and sideways comments. "While you all were busily saving two by two animals and your own sorry bottoms I had other cosmic issues confronting me, remember?"

"Like what?" Queries Falc, his ever super ego back in full attack mode, even if it is God.

God. "Ah, yes this demonstrates another problem with you single minded earthlings. You think everything revolves around you, wait till Galileo shows up. But during your 'once in a lifetime' cruise I had to wrestle with a bevy of far out galaxies bent on bumping into each other just for the ducks of it. On top of these out in space rebellions I also had a testy problem with a bunch of vociferous black holes popping up everywhere trying to consume each other. Their personalities are almost like tiny human sailors. At the other end of the "size spectrum" there is a bunch of string like creepy crawlers kicking sand in each other's face. This G.d. – oops – universe management job is stressing me – understand? So cool it, Falc. Noah is right; you are an ark hitch hiker and not one of the selected few so watch your words."

Falc sulks from God's rebuke, but realizes some gratitude and sympathy is called for.

God continues unloading more of his personal issues. "That is not all, just when these unearthly problems are confronting me, my beautiful golden long haired, blue eyed poopsy Goddess decides to have her face lifted, nose bobbed and while at it replant some slightly yellowed and crooked teeth. Have you ever tried working with self appointed cosmic skin and bone doctors, who employ weirdo lawyers, all whose sole greedy life objective is playing golf and making money? Just getting appointments with these clowns was a nightmare. Shish."

"However, my biggest conundrum the whole time you were at sea was how did so many creatures escape my big drown? They surely weren't on the ark with you, where they? What it means is that there still may remain major flaws in the universe." God's words taper off as he shakes his head in disbelief. "Maybe next time I should resort to a Texas style western barbeque, where everything goes up in smoke and flames."

"Gee whiz God, We surely are deeply sorry for all these challenges you faced while we were merrily enjoying our leisure time afloat and playing sea games. You really should have come along. If you had, we could all have been drinking good wine instead of rutabaga beer. But face it, your Goddess really looks chic with all those alterations." Chirps the ever flamboyant Hummy.

"Time out." commands Captain Noah. "All this self pity and teasing crap won't help us renovate the ark to become wind powered and steerable. It is high time to demonstrate to the world that we are seasoned nautical engineers and sailors, bent on improving our seafaring lives through experience, cooperative efforts and proven technologies." Refurbishing begins in earnest. To celebrate God suddenly uncorks some vintage wines he just concocted. "Wow is this good stuff." They all agree.

Everyone takes a personal breather realizing that the recent cruise did not eliminate worldly ego problems. Falc is privately reminiscing about his former human tamer Mustafa, who should by now be properly history, but then again maybe not. If Hummy is right, he might just be a high roller living it up in the desert. Mustafa was clever. I must look him up – he may just be rich.

A theological moment arises. Falc begins the discussion by asking God if he really thinks there might possibly be other gods out there that have contributed to His many irksome personal problems. "As I see it God, you may have some serious competition for top billing, but again maybe it is just a figment of a paranoid imagination. Perhaps your Big KaBoom really had a few minor flaws that weren't immediately recognized. If that is the case, we need to concoct a foolproof cosmic security system. You know, metal detectors, passport control, take off your sandals and all that legal stuff to insure potential alien god followers are not admitted to our new ark before the next drowning. Have you ever considered pre-emptive drowning?" Falc can be tough.

Captain Noah begins to realize that things haven't changed all that much after the big soak. "Listen up you guys. I too, have been thinking seriously about our recent rainstorm consequences. We luckily survived thanks to you God Almighty. And so here we all sit; you God, me a wretched human, and two seasoned smart derriere bird arkers on a no longer derelict leaky scow, drinking Your newly vintage wines and discussing cruising to warmer climates where voluptuous and nubile females of all species abound. We must be thankful, don't you think? I surely hope we don't have to readdress fig leaves and apple issues."

"Absolutely true Captain Noe. And let me assure you conditions aren't so dire that we have to resort to learning algebra, probability and chaos theory, of which we surely have all had enough." Responds God. "But Falc, you may be on to something regarding a multitude of amateur wanna-a-be Gods mischievously provoking me in my own universe. Your observations might account for some of the un-Godly commotion that has been occurring like, you know, the worms and black holes. Also please do elaborate on your CSS (Cosmic Security System) ideas. This idea is worth pursuing."

The discussion intensifies on the topic of multiple Gods vying for positions of power by exerting as yet poorly understood influences throughout the universe. God is both engaged and enraged at the thought he may have competitors. Security does become a major concern. "How many dimensions do think there are Hummy?"

These cosmic problems are now perceived as much graver issues than having to drown a bunch of misbehaving earthly inhabitants. "As I reflect back on all the different groupings of warring folks that evolved, each did come up with their own god or bunch of gods. This godly cloning possibility may help explain all the heavenly competition I face." Opines a deeply troubled and confused God. "I should have included all those upstart gods in My shower and then sent them to hell to warm up and dry out forever." God is not viewed as a patsy by the other arkers.

Falc on a thoughtful role asks God. "Why are you surprised at there being so many gods? Let's face it, you god's exist in a tax free bull market. This is bound to create return on investment competition, which should be economically healthy - definitely Econ 101 stuff."

"Geesus God, just an aside here to relieve Your stress, did You ever think of having some kids?" Inquires Hummy. "That way You could expand Your personal Godly influences, you know, 'God Associates'. As Your kids mature You could take some vacations and enjoy God grandkids. However, be warned that their teen years might be a challenge for You, especially when they get the hang of making good wine from bad water."

"Hummy, you are an inquisitive kind and yes indeed the Goddess and I have discussed having a family, but there are some touchy issues that We have not been able to agree on; so for the moment, it is a great idea and I hope We can soon work out the details. I really would just love being a God daddy and grand daddy. My thoughts are to outsource the job so the Missus wouldn't have to be burdened with all those usual baby feeding and pooping issues, you know. I do have a guy by the name of Joe in mind if he ever gets around to sparking his girl friend Mary. Perhaps I can really shake folks up by having a son smarter and nicer than everyone." Replies God, wistfully.

Noah senses this cosmology and family discussion may lead to considerable inaction on the immediate need to continue renovating the ark in preparation for a long cruise. Again Noah announces a decision. "We will sail westward as soon as final touches are made to the ark. Let us all get busy. We can more easily resolve tricky metaphysical and child rearing issues while sailing." Still true today.

"Indulge me for just another second." Pleads God. "If I do have other Godly or un-Godly competitors, what should be my approach; should I try to partner with them, duke it out or simply cop out and have kids and let evolution take care of the details, please help me."

Falc. "Duke it out God, we are right behind you, I can skillfully remove both godly and ungodly eyeballs - so they won't see a thing. Gives you a real punching advantage,"

Hummy, who was restless but silent throughout the discussions on cosmology, now feels an impulse to put this topic to rest and get on with sailing westward. "Good God Almighty, You surely know that I too have deep compassion for all Your multi-challenging dilemmas. But to address Your specific question on what to do, I differ completely with Falc. Yes, there probably are an endless number of approaches, but a God led beer bar brawl fisticuff with your godly competitors is surely not a sociably acceptable option for someone in Your position, especially after You recently drowned everyone else for being overly aggressive. And if You do have a kid or a bunch - that is really bad karma for little children."

Hummy continues. "So before You start a brouhaha over who is top God, I suggest it be prudent for You to first take a leisurely romantic cruise, relax and sort out details. Take the Missus, some good wine and frilly nightwear. You know that the four of us, Noah, Sarah, Falc and me are deeply devoted to You and will certainly assist in whatever manner we can. You can easily justify this cruising caper by presenting a strategic motivational leadership seminar on the positive benefits of drowning. No one will have any inkling what that is all about, but it sounds OK. Keep in mind that as good arker-sailors it behooves us to put off everything important and first go sailing. So keep that thought in mind."

"Right on Hummy. Our motto is; sail first and if later on time permits take care of the universes' business." Chimes First Mate Falc. "God I hope you realize that You have here really great supportive buddies, on the sea and in the universe."

"You are right Falc, we may disagree but we are right behind you God." adds Hummy.

God, bewildered and overwhelmed with so many well meant and loving suggestions is shaking his head in humble disbelief. "It is certainly a blessing to have so many good buddies, thank you all."

Noah, seeking action, has now figured out that he can build something called a sail, based on Falc's clever idea. That bird is clever; he even knows how to take the square root of a number like four. God quickly assists in rigging the sail by performing some power miracles in procuring exotic materials and provide muscle for the heavy lifting.

"But what about the two shoppers, especially my Goddess, aren't they going to be perturbed when they return with their extravagant purchases and see the ark sailing gaily away on the horizon - Pacific Isle bound?" Wonders God aloud so they can all hear him. "How long can they keep up their shopping frenzy, now in its seventh day?"

"Not to worry mates - females can shop forever." Rasps the every teasing Falc.

The once lumbering smelly ark is rapidly becoming a work of beauty thanks to God's do-it-yourself miracles. The ark's majestic white sails gracefully flutter from local off shore zephyrs that signal an eagerness to propel the ark to faraway tropical islands. The heavy keel has greatly added stability to the formerly tippy "canoe" ark. These additions make the ark no longer a simply direction-less ark, but rather an ocean seaworthy sailing yacht. God, Noah, Hummy and Falc are proud as new fathers. But Noah is secretly wondering where in hell was God when he Noah was busily making the first ark by hauling logs over sand dunes? Hmmm.

Concerns linger about what the Goddess and her shopping companion Sarah will think - if and when they return and find the ark gone. Captain Noe reminds his buddies that the ladies did demand they clean up the ark before they left. "Right? We did as told and we are now simply on a sea trial."

"Just relax mates, that is the price females pay for shopping and males pay for fixing the ark so we can go back to sea." Reminds Falc with a distinct Hawaiian lilt in his voice and blatant disregard for God's veiled guilty sentiments. The falcon has no intention of going back to flying over hot dusty deserts looking for scrawny mite infested mice for lunch, when a life at sea can be spent swaying, singing, imbibing and wondering how many gods there really are in the universe. Every sailor's dream.

With a masculine sense of bravado and abandonment the foursome continue to make plans to shove off. Sails are billowing; the rigging is standing erect and taut while the rudder responds deftly to Captain Noah's slightest efforts. Again Chantilly songs can be heard as they fine tune their voices in a naval quartet. God has produced an abundance of fine port wines, all are working as a team and so at this moment their futures are looking pretty darn good.

"Hear ye, hear ye. We must immediately set sail straight away for the warm South Pacific islands." squeaks the enthusiastic Hummy. God did not enter into the; hear ye, hear te, rah-rah; since he is still mulling issues of celestial leadership and property rights and the possibility of becoming a pop.

In the meantime, the Goddess and Sarah, who earlier had high tailed it to the malls to model the latest fashions, are still there and totally oblivious to what has happened on the renovated New Age Ark. Has the big rain storm really changed clothing styles, colors and odors, is their primary concern? "Don't you just love those pointy shoes with their spiked heels Sarah?" Coos the Goddess as she gingerly stuffs her size 12 triple "E" feet into a pair of red pumps - "Oooh, la la".

"I just wished I had had a pair of them on the cruise, they would have been my weapon of choice against those pesky forever sniffing male animals." Replies Sarah. "I am going to get six pairs, each a different color, just in case we have to repeat our last escapade."

Goddess. "Don't be silly Sarah, God and I will never again resort to drowning. I think everyone has by now learned a valuable lesson to be nice and respectful of each other. Our new future Garden of Eden will be a truly peaceful haven where we females can shop eternally and those uncouth males can play with their sailboats in warm clear waters while drinking bad beer. Just for fun though, we may stick a couple of orca sharks in the tank to keep them on their toes. Furthermore there will be lots of slithering asps to tempt us ladies. Hee-Hee."

Falc, who is fully committed to getting off shore, abruptly and out of the blue, begins orating eloquently on the concept of freedom and personal rights. "Freedom is what it is all about. Isn't that why we have wars? Being free means you can do whatever the hell turns your fancy as long as you are tough enough and have the money. It is our duty to explore new vistas and conquer new lands, in our beautiful yacht. With God on our side we are bound to dominate everyone. Freedom is our godly entitlement, right, God?"

Hummy too, likes the notion of unfettered liberty. "Right on Falc, let's raise the burgees, cut the mooring lines and get this ark- a-sailing. Freedom forever is our bird motto."

Noah and God shake their heads but remain silent. They sense a déjà vu future.

God is psychologically stressed realizing that His big drown has not really changed the nature of earthly animals. He is also facing a multitude of serious issues, but three are serious, a) My heavenly bodies have taken off on a seemingly uncontrolled self-destructive tack, b).The unnerving notion of having godly competition, and c) My apparently limited math skills. They now intersect producing a perfect cosmic chaos.

For icing on this cake, I hear this nonsensical mantra about unfettered freedom coming from two drunken birds that allegedly and gleefully discovered My computational error in determining rainfall. "Alas, where, oh where did I go so, so wrong; or was it really the damn fig leafs the Goddess insisted on having Adam and Eve wear in the Garden? Maybe poison sumac would have been a better choice."

Falc. "You know what God? You and the misses truly tried many unproven techniques to rein in the unwholesome behavior of your creatures; you tried art, threats of hell and damnation, and now drowning. Did you ever consider humor? Get folks laughing and they will immediately see the folly of killing each other, instead they will die laughing and everyone will be dead happy, eh? You and all your wanna-be gods should become stand up comics. Just a weird suggestion."

However, God takes this flippant idea seriously. "Why didn't I think of that earlier? Great idea Falc, My universe is a joke."

Noah's Ark, responding to stronger gusts of wind, begins moving ever so slowly, but majestically, away from the shore. It floats high in the water now that the creatures have either gone to town or taken off to make whoopee in the hinterlands. After all that was their duty following the cruise and they are dutifully obeying.

In this post flood era it appears life on earth is again settling back into shopping, procreating and sailing.

From the bridge, God, Noah, Falc and Hummy notice that some of the large meat eaters are racing back towards the ark. Snarling lions, tigers, cheetahs and panthers are leading the pack, followed by a parade of grunting rhinos and laughing hyenas. They are obviously deeply concerned about being late for their now well established and traditional beer drinking happy hour on the ark. The foursome onboard arker's faces become ashen. "Heave away mates, before it is too late - we are short on beer and the carnivore drinkers are headed home to the bar! yells Captain Noah."

Falc is panicking at the helm as his efforts to steer and direct the ark respond ever so slowly, as every sailor knows will happen whenever you are in a tight spot. The ark is barely moving. Hummy, now hovering high overhead is screeching details on the location of the impending invasion of the beer thirsty meat eaters. The ark's security situation is elevated from orange to red.

"We need more wind! Blow!" yells Captain Noe.

In response to Noah's orders for more wind the ark strangely begins moving faster. The helm responds smartly as Falc deftly steers the ark westward towards the open rolling sea. The ark is picking up speed to the point that there is no way the thundering happy hour seekers can catch them.

Captain Noah is flabbergasted. "What in the world is going on? Who is in charge here?" He realizes that he, Noah the Captain, had absolutely nothing to do with the changing wind conditions and is confused, but greatly relieved.

God sits quietly, nursing his port, with a grin wide as all out doors, thinking to himself, "I have performed yet another miracle, making it three in a row, big bang, big flood, big blow. Not bad for an old well meaning nice guy with limited math skills, eh?" His thrashed ego is slowly repairing itself as he again exerts his Godly powers. The sea will do this – time and again.

The Goddess is scoring equally big with Sarah, her bosom shopping and champagne guzzling partner. They are still madly dashing from mall to mall, like fireflies drawn to flaming candles, seeking out the latest fashions in shoes, panties and bras. They are greeted with more great news, all the shops will from now on remain open twenty-four, seven. Word of the Noah cruise passengers coming ashore has gotten to all the merchants who can't wait to accommodate them. The muskrats just love having their fur washed, rinsed and set. All the animals just love receiving personal attention.

Sarah suggests to the Goddess they get hotel rooms for the night. "I would surely like to take an aromatic soak to ease my swollen feet and aching back. I will get a head to toe body aromatic massage and have my hair done before hopping into these beautiful clothes I bought. Wow, I wish Noah could see me now!"

"Great idea Sarah." Responds the Goddess as she checks her credit card limit.

In the meantime, the New Noah's Ark, is now fully under sail heading towards tropical islands. They are on a beam reach under a stiff breeze. The ark is manned by four exceedingly happy arkers, God, Noah, Falc and Hummy, each seeking new frontiers. These formerly beer drinking males are basking in their freedom and happiness, or so they hope. Hummy, who is a smart little bird with a keen sense of smell is, in spite of his small snooty, pointy beak, screeching out headings for Falc to steer.

Just maybe - humming birds are the ones in charge of the universe. "I tell straight on fellow humans – you are and remain the missing links – stop looking - sorry." Chirps Hummy as he directs their beautiful ark towards warm seas and fair winds.

"God, you sure do know how to pull off big plays in spite of your overwhelming personal tribulations. How do you do it?" Asks Captain Noah contently seated in his voluminous leather captain's chair on the bridge.

"Noe, what I like about you is just about everything. Yes indeed, I do have earthly and heavenly problems that you can't imagine. Big sky issues are almost like the problems I had with you inane earthlings. Everyone is leading a grubby avarice life of their own, feeling they are entitled to whatever they want. I sometimes feel I have lost ultimate control." God again begins to sink into despondency as he realizes how much of his universe may no longer be under his thumb, but he still gets the blame for all the problems. "Can't we all just somehow get along? Anyone have a good joke to tell?"

"Wow-ee. If You aren't in control God, then who in the h.... is?" Noah almost uses that "h" word again. Was it possible Falc's earlier comments on multiple gods had really rattled the Big Guy? Wonders Noah.

Captain Noah decides to again try to perk up God' low spirits. "God, I really think you need to do this motivational style cruise we suggested. You would energize us all with your vision for the future as God, indeed the NOG (Number One God). You could use this spacious ark, deliver homilies, produce sample deluges interspersed with fire and brimstone demos."

Scare the bejeesus out of naughty politicians, doctors and lawyers who legally cruise solely as a creative tax dodge. Your old fashioned revival style presentations, backed with our enthusiastic testimonies and clever power point displays, would boost your currently sagging reviews among the "other" gods. Sarah and I can both help you based on our arking experiences on how to take two by two of every species for a once in a life time sea voyage based simply on the need to avoid drowning. I can just see the promo banners and tee shirts – ***Boost Your Sales (Sails) by Staying Alive While Arking;*** or perhaps more to the point, ***Arking Prevents Drowning*** and so it is, ***Ark or Drown***. We will package these provocative inspirational slogans as statements approved by You God, e.g. ***"I have read and approve this ad – God Almighty."*** Future political parties will love this.

It is now God and Noah's turn to wax and wane on heavy issues.

"Thanks, Noe, I appreciate your desire to help. I, the God Almighty, have also been wondering ever since his big shower, who really is in charge of the universe. According to My biographer guy whom I never knew very well, named King Jim, I created every creature and all matter – and it was good. What rankles Me is who or what is creating all this upset and conflict throughout what I thought was My Universe? I am possessive you know. Falc's conjecture of a bunch of godless gods loose in the cosmos is for sure most unsettling. What about this anti-matter stuff swooshing around causing cosmic mayhem, giving Me personal headaches and heartaches. This all because there are a bunch of meany ungodly gods and that I didn't do well in algebra? You really never know where your problems can come from, do you?"

Hummy is stoically thinking to himself, ah yes, the power of algebra, a lot of humans don't get it. It is truly a truism: ***Algebra or die.***

"Now if there is someone else challenging my authority, who is it, could it be my old nemeses, that devil with his fork and tail?" God continues softly muttering somewhat incoherently to himself, "I thought I drowned everyone, including him, but already your wife and my Goddess are back in the malls consuming like crazy, while us males are headed to the South Seas in search of skirts. All my cleverly created stuff in the sky refuses to sit still and twinkle. My saved two-by-two non-human animals have taken off to indulge themselves. Don't patronize me Noe ole buddy, but isn't this a big Tums moment? Alas, I think I will get myself another rutabaga beer instead of this expensive merlot. Good ole warm rutabaga beer really does clarify my thinking. Someday I must visit this place called Askov, they deserve to be recognized as the Rutabaga Capitol of the Universe."

"Ten degrees to port then straight ahead." shouts Hummy. What he isn't telling his mates is that he is fantasying about the sweet scent of verdant flora a-blooming in far away isles. Instinctively he knows that where there are sweet lush blossoms you always find gorgeous screeching female hummingbirds. His mind has conjured up visions of tall coconut trees lining sandy beaches, being lulled to sleep by the sound of gently warm azure blue ocean waves, and so on. Hummy intends to steer God's new ark there.

Falc has been quietly organizing his thoughts and now addresses God. "God, I certainly believe in you being omniscient and omnipotent, although your limited math skills challenge the omniscience factor. However, there is absolutely no question that you are all powerful, as witnessed by your making this big pond that we arked around in forever. So here is my question based on your power factor. Why don't you simply make all your Black Holes spin backwards, thereby spewing back all the cosmic stuff they have been swallowing? That would wind your time clock into the past. Then stop this rewind process just before the fig leaf skivvy dropping fad began and before anyone had taken a bite out of any apples. At this point some systemic intervention therapy could be initiated. Bingo - all would again be well in The Garden and we would be back to square one."

God. "You know Falc, I wish you had been around in those days, you certainly have succinct, and uncluttered ideas about solving complex issues. I should not beat myself up but it seems that lately I am often being a day late and a nickel short."

As Noah's New Ark sails smartly towards the now darkening bluish western skies each crew member begins privately fantasizing about their future. Sailing does that, it opens new mental passages into your own imperfect inner world.

Hummy is considering taking up oil painting scenes of himself in aerobatic flight. Humming birds are artistically gifted, sensitive, and have a great sense of humor. They tend to use all bright colors throughout their art work, but especially reds.

Falc is really only pseudo tough, he lies when convenient, drinks moderately to heavy, very touchy about his rear feathers and thinks deeply about the pure and universal truths. He is becoming an Emmanuel Kant, as in Critique of Pure Bird-dom. However, practically Falc sees his future focused on learning to crack fresh coconuts, fly aerobatics and all the while searching for the meaning of life through humor.

Noah, drifting into a soft dreamy world, is finally appreciating his own leadership talents, considers opening a major entertainment venue based on his arking experiences. This ark park would include many water related rides and an aviary full of falcons and hummingbirds teaching each other to fly. Privately Noah begins basking in knowing he successfully negotiated with God and His Goddess, built an ark in the desert, loaded it with nubile animals, sailed it aimlessly without mishap, and is now contemplating entering the entertainment industry. This all began when a simple first time boater– arker obeyed God's need to clean up a troubled planet. A full life indeed! For the moment sleep softly envelops everyone on Noah's Ark, including Noah.

God is fiendishly working on the concept of making his universe a cosmic comedy show, where big jokes will replace all other previous big projects. I must have a talk with the hyenas, who already seem to enjoy laughing.

CHAPTER 12

CELESTIAL BAR AND GRILL

The second day of sea trials for the refurbished ark goes extremely well. All the ark systems function beautifully under ideal weather conditions. The crew is enthusiastic and in synch – as least nautically. Their personal objectives remain varied and spirited.

The single overarching philosophical issue that God and Noah's ark saga failed to answer is; who is in charge of the universe? There are arguably three possibilities to consider; no one, everyone or some finite number in between. God still clings to being the only number one.

Nonetheless it would appear that the fearless cosmologists falcon and a restless artsy hummingbird may to be on to something, but it would take more time for them to clearly construct a finalized Unifying Theory of Godness (UTG), since arking-sailing is just too much fun to get too serious. But the question begs answering. How many gods are there?

As night again engulfs the crew in nocturnal reverie the beautifully refurbished ark slips effortlessly through the night sky now brilliant with glorious heavenly displays. The newly redesigned ark's characteristics include self-steering capabilities, a fine wine cellar, odor free holding tank plumbing, concert hall music and a moderately drinking crew dedicated to having fun while deciphering the universe and sharing thoughts with God. Throughout the night the ark slogs faithfully towards an as yet undisclosed future landfall. For the moment there exists a pervasive and deep ephemeral serenity found only on expertly designed and well crewed arks. This is truly the epitome of sailing.

Periodically during the night God Almighty is restless with His agonizing universal predicaments. Finally, He silently reenters the bridge, gets a beer and starts some serious thinking. It is now a given that His epic events have had some flaws. The Ka-boom was a dreadful failure; the Garden of Eden led to this unparallel drowning event followed by a landing that seems to be marginal efficacious, perhaps leading to another catastrophically debacle. I just must learn from My mistakes and My dear friends.

God begins analyzing what is going on while actually enjoying the whoopee noises echoing in the far away hills – the planet is again alive. He wonders about his Goddess and Sarah shopping endlessly again consuming more than earth can possibly afford while Noah and his two bird buddies dream about warm winds and waters in the South Pacific. They are also fantasizing about ways to run the universe's clock backwards by unwinding black holes. Finally there is the ever nagging possibility of multiple deities and their unpredictable antics. God is faced with the fact that things have really not changed a whole lot since Noah's ark cruise began, except he has met a couple of really nice birds. "I must come up with a new Godly plan."

As night slips effortlessly into dawn God struggles to find yet another solution.

Far away a beautiful morning sky opens rapidly with a palette of brilliant colorful, flashing and bubbling unnamed but beautiful cosmic stuff. The stars begin twinkling less brightly as the sun takes command and produces yet another gorgeous day for those at sea. Sunrise at sea is always spectacular. The ark's crew is shaking off their last nocturnal nautical dreams while the shoppers, Goddess and Sarah, are still at it in the shops of endless "can't live without it" bargains.

Big bang, big drown, big ark, big malls. What will be the next big biggy? Only God knows and He is now about to reveal it. Quietly He asks his slowly awakening crew to "please gather around."

"Oh oh" they mutter as a sense of grave uncertainly befalls them.

God clears his throat. "Captain Noe, Falc and Hummy; let Me share with you what I decided last night while alone in the bridge drinking rutabaga beer, which I still really enjoy." Begins God in a soft, but confident voice.

Look out - here it comes. Think Noah, Falc and Hummy. This is not going to bode well for our anticipated South Pacific 'chick cruise'. "Sure God, of course we are most eager to hear about your new plan. Do tell."

"Okay. First things first - I must confess that as Falc alluded to earlier, there may indeed be a whole bunch of us Gods vying for control of the universe. The signs are seemingly everywhere. All those rich fired up hell and damnation preachers, sullen arrogant gurus sitting on mountain peaks along with street fakers and their snakes are surely indicative that I may indeed have serious competition. All these holy wars in the names of star struck gods are really upsetting Me. But since I am The true God of peace and love I have decided on a totally different approach by taking the high ground that will forever insure my dominance and put an end to religious wars and long dull convoluted sin sermons."

"Hallelujah, and what is that God?" Chirps the wide eyed nervous now fully awake Hummy.

"By all means do tell us." Adds Noah as he uneasily reflects back to a time that now seems long ago, when early one morning God came into his modest tent and suggested drowning most everybody. The ante has now been raised; this time God is taking on all the gods that be.

We are going to need a much bigger ark thinks Noah - Wow-ee.

The always leery Falc keeps his beak shut waiting for more information, but also senses this may not be great news for birds.

God speaks. "You have all taught me an important lesson about drowning the folks I can't tolerate. Arguably it just did not work. Thus, there will be no more mega ka-booms or monstrous drownings; this time I and the missus will open – now hear this clearly - The God and Goddess's Celestial Bar and Grill to be known simply as the CB&G. We will cultivate in every one who attends a desire for harmony, peace, tolerance, trust, mutual respect and healthy lifestyles through humor. This time big-ka-boom and mass drowning will be superseded to become the Big Funny", thereby reducing the fear and stress level we are all facing. We need ludicrous cosmic jokes and CB&G will be the place to tell them."

"Ya-Hoo." Screeches Falc, who now mightily supports God's earlier comments about taking a very different approach. "A Celestial Bar and Grill of this magnitude will surely bring the universe together, merrily and joyfully. You are indeed omniscient God. All these other challenging gods will clearly be embarrassed by their warped personalities as they start telling bad jokes at the CB&G. As we all know it is physically impossible for anyone, except politicians and lawyers, to be nasty when they are laughing. Fantastic idea, God!"

"Yes, that is right Falc. We will open up as the true and only cosmos watering hole, a celestial oasis, where all the Gods, Goddesses, arkers, sailors and wanna-be whatever are welcomed to meet, share good humor. You Noah, will be the architect, contractor and facility manager; so - make this edifice look like a gigantic celestial ark. Falc, you will be in charge of keeping the place orderly and insure all philosophical discussions are honest, under control, but above all funny. Hummy, you will do the public relations chores. Go spread the word." God is all smiles and pleased – the first time in a very long while. He can't wait to get started.

God continues. "I emphasize that the key is humor – keep em laughing. We will have all these amateur upstart gods do daily standup comic gigs. Each week there will be a Heavenly Hilarity Contest (HHC) and the one that wins will be crowned the Funny God of the Week (FGW). Remember, all the jokes must be pure and clean - no naughty words, violence or sex. However, political and lawyer jokes are especially encouraged.

"What about some musical entertainment?" Queries Falc who realizes joke boredom could easily set in and then everyone would begin to squabble over issues like how much to tithe the best jokester or, should there be an imposed value added joke tax? As we know taxes are often not seen as jokes."

"You are right, Falc. Tithing and tax issues are touchy topics. But My Goddess, always humble and modest, is really an excellent country western contralto singer and I am sure she will be thrilled to add musical zip for the comedians jokes. I can't wait to tell her." adds God.

Noah. "Hey God, wait a minute guys, my Sarah is great on flute, lute and zither. The two of them will be a dynamite duet. Bedeck their gorgeous bodies with flashy spangles and dangles, prop them up on red stiletto heels, add a pointy dunce type hat with cotton balls and they will become knock 'em dead cosmic hooters. Oh, dear, dear me, this is really getting to be honest to goodness fun. It surely beats drowning."

Captain Noah continues. "It is settled then. My stomach is not taking this sea life well either, so we will now turn the ark around, head back to the quay and begin making new plans. When the ladies finally come back from shopping we will startle them with My next Big production – The Celestial Bar and Grill – where the future is a joke."

God is happy as a clam, just like he was when he picked Noah for the ark episode. "This guy Noah really knows how to command." Noah too, is emotionally willing to forego, at least for the moment, another lengthy sea voyage. He reasons that future day sailing will keep his nautical skills current and allow him time to develop CB&G. He, like God, is always ecstatic about new challenges and opportunities.

Finally the Goddess and Sarah return to the ark, exhausted, yet exuberant over their many purchases. They had never even suspected their crew mates had been out for a glorious ark sea trial and made momentous decisions that would forever alter their course of heavenly and earthly futures.

As they enter the ark the Goddess says, "Sarah you are one great shopper. We must do this again and again. Look at all this beautiful stuff; I especially love my diamond broche. God will be tickled at how it twinkles, just like my eyes. And I can't wait for a report on Noah's reaction to your Victoria underwear purchases. Tee-Hee."

"You know what, Goddess, Noah may just drop over dead when he sees me in these provocative duds. We sure did have fun shopping. Wonder what the rover boys and their two dim witted birds did while we were gone. For sure they did clean and fix up our ark; it doesn't even look like the old one anymore. It smells sooo good. Wonder where everyone is?"

"Surprise and welcome home ye intrepid shoppers." shout God and Noah as they burst into the refurbished bridge. "Tell us all about your commercial ventures that have further depleted the planet."

The planetary depletion comment did not register on anyone. Interests centered on the sheer joy of conspicuous consumption.

"Oh God, dear God, look at this diamond, isn't it just the biggest rock you every saw? Yells the excited Goddess. And look at the nighties Sarah got, as she holds up what appears to be mostly air." Sure enough Noah fainted dead away.

Falc and Hummy are delirious with laughter commenting: "One buys a big shiny rock while the other gets see through drawers. It is too much I tell you." Noah quickly recovers and goes looking for beer thinking perhaps they should not have returned from their intended sail to the South Pacific. But too late now.

God truly hopes that his new plan will be the final and eternal solution. "I need a break."

The Goddess and Sarah continue talking incessantly and sharing their purchases; God, Noah, Falc and Hummy are discussing their aborted short sail westward and how lucky they all are to again being together on the bridge of their renovated ark.

With enthusiasm God takes the center stage announcing. "Listen up everyone, a momentous decision has been made; I am again the God of My universe."

"Oh no God, no, no please." Laments Sarah. "Just when everything is working so well; we ladies have a great mega mall with outlets galore and you guys have a gorgeous polished teak trimmed ark with a two birdbrain crew, why can't we just call it nirvana and stop making more confused masculine ka-boom decisions? Let me tell you one thing for sure, dearest beloved God Almighty, Much as I adore you I will not be a party to any more big-bangs, fiery hells or big drown-outs. The future for us ladies is big box shops full of stuff, dig it? Why do all you arker- sailor types always behave like the perennial independent thinking lemmings booming off to somewhere?" Sarah is wound up and determined that no new God plan is going to interfere with her life. "I have suffered too, much too much."

The ark goes silent as everyone looks at their shoe laces.

"No, No Sarah. Hear me out. My latest decision is just what is needed at this time in history. I am opening up – now get this - The God and Goddess's Celestial Bar and Grill. This will become the replacement for all My former less than successful colossal K-type events. It will be a haven, indeed a gigantic heaven, where all the Gods, Goddesses, fakers, arkers, sailors and mall hoppers can regularly congregate; tell jokes, sing karaoke led by you and the Goddess. Furthermore you can share deep happy thoughts, eat vitamin laced veggie burgers, drink fresh healthy apple juice and/or authentic Askovian rutabaga hooch. How glorious is that?

Wait there is more, in addition to The Celestial Bar & Grill; we will have a mega gold souk on one corner of the Cosmic One Avenue, an Arker-boat outlet on the other and a gaudy casino across the street.

Finally, to top it all off, I will open up The Bird Brain Academy for Higher Order Thinking Skills. This will honor serious thinkers, especially mathematicians and will be staffed by our own two gifted bird arker companions, Falc and Hummy." God is exuberant.

"Hallelujah", screech Hummy and Falc, "We birds have finally been recognized as the intellectually superior species and given our own higher education operation. Thanks, God"

"Oh for God's sake, oops, you will do what God? Best you cut out the higher order gibberish that could again lead to a repeat of what went wrong before; as you yourself said we now need fun." Snaps the now itchy want-a-go-shopping Goddess. She and Sarah have bonded. "You guys are good to get your jollies on boats, junk yards and casinos. But Sarah and I are destined to shop. You want a real dust-up – just try your hand at deterring ladies from going to the malls."

Oooh. The Big Funny is in trouble.

Hummy can't wait to enter the discussion. "See, I told you all this Sin City stuff I visited had these exact essentials; boats, bars and casinos for guys with gold and scanty clothes shops for females. Everyone enjoyed telling jokes; some were a tad tawdry, if you know what I mean. I tell you it is a match made in heaven: Ladies shop, guys sail, and birds think."

God wistfully smiles realizing the His cosmos is moving in a new jovial direction under his leadership, but also accepting the fact that he has no viable alternative suggestions. "What about my higher order thinking Academy? Maybe I will have to settle for a small corner reading room, stocked with comic and a few math puzzle books."

God and Noah, finally begin to worry about thinking skills being ruled out for humans and replaced by the birds to do all the mental chores. This really smacks of outsourcing human mental activities to the birds. Will humans ever learn? Probably not!

The Happy Hour that followed on Noah's beautifully polished teak and poshly outfitted ark was genuinely spirited. While the initial post deluge landing experience of a few days ago had been confusing to say the least, this celebration was truly euphoric. Everyone had stories and wild ideas to share about their futures. Sarah began telling sailor jokes and singing cruising songs accompanied by the Goddess on lutes, flutes and zithers. Periodically Noah had to exert some minor censorship. Their futures looked promising indeed while the drowned masses were quickly forgotten.

God, always generous and helpful, believed that if he could surround Himself with all the challenging gods in a relaxed atmosphere of good food and libation, remove any profit motive and stress the humor of it all, he could convincingly prove that he was The In-charge God. Then by all pooling their perceived heavenly resources, and with God's leadership, they could collectively control the universe and tackle the dark physics conundrums of the day. Following that, many Gardens of Eden could flourish together peacefully, each supporting and sponsoring competitive sporting teams. These cosmic cup events would become known as The Cosmic Playoff Cup Series (CPCS), hosted by current and former arkers. The universe would then once and for all be rid of black holes, stock markets and genuine crooks allowing everyone endless time for laughing, giggling and arking/sailing.

Another nightfall begins on Noah's beautiful and nearly empty ark. Animals, two by two, are still joyfully cavorting in the newly dried out sand dunes as the natural order returns. The God and Goddess have slipped unnoticed up to their heavenly abode. Noah and Sarah are snuggled together overwhelmed by all the good luck that has befallen them. Falc and Hummy are aggressively yakking on the bridge about who will be the provost of their Bird Brain Academy and what will be admission standards. They tend towards requiring an ad infinitum set of multiple choice algebra tests, thereby insuring students will die before completion, thus no failures, only deaths. Many years later this nutty notion was adopted by colleges and universities everywhere. "Keep flunking em.".

There is no more rain. The storm has passed and the desert is again dry - for now.

But alas, the ubiquitous Black Holes still spin in a clockwise or counter clockwise direction (depending on your orientation) and indiscernible slippery worms creep unrestrained throughout Bohr's whirling atoms. Has anyone learned anything from this watery saga? Yes indeed, hope still springs eternal in every arker/sailor's breast and with one unwavering objective; go sailing. And when you get your ark-boat safely back to port, moor it and enjoy the beach with its excited inhabitants - you are truly a Noah Winner.

Without doubt Captain Noah did successfully establish nautical standards and maritime behavioral trends for the future, based solidly on experiences learned as a first time arker/boater in a drowning world. But he wished he knew more mathematics. We are not sure just what knowledge was gained, but it is a good bet we ought to pay more attention to our behavior patterns, which now includes telling jokes and laughing heartily.

The Big Funny has begun.

KUDOS & WHERE ARE THEY NOW

It is thanks to Noah – that today cosmology, religion, metaphysics and ark-boating have all become premiere mental activities for non-thinking animals, most often males. Noah now manages a hi-tech ark-yacht sales agency and The Celestial Bar and Grill, where all the Gods that be, arkers, sailors and restless thinkers irreligiously convene at happy hour - which begins daily at about noon - has become the official center of the universe. All drinks are on the house. Noah opens each session with a heavenly joke, often badly told, but applauded out of respect for his past achievements. He day-sails almost weekly.

We wish Noah well.

Thanks to Sarah, everyone survived the arduous life of living on a homemade ark where new social mores were developed with neurotic passengers whose sole life purpose was daily survival. Following her sea saga Sarah became a tycoon in establishing gargantuan global malls and souks that are today's ultimate shopping playgrounds, most often for women. Privately she operates "The Heavenly Psycho Chandlery". Her current publications are comic books specializing in *"Neo Clinical Psychology for Ark Bound Animals"* and *"How to Effectively Placate Grumpy Sailors without Beer"*. Her grumpy sailor research tends to indicate this is impossible. However, neither of her publication has yet made the best seller list.

We wish Sarah well.

Special thanks to God and Goddess, of course. They had the clear vision to select strong characters like Noah and Sarah, who became the sole role models for today's humankind; following the drowning of everyone else. What God and Goddesses will do next, if we don't all behave, is pure speculation. We can only believe that comic success at The Celestial Bar and Grill is our best hope for a better future – should be a hoot.

God, who remains very cerebral, moralistic and now also a humorist is debating on retaking a developmental algebra course, tacking on a lesson or two in probability and Chaos Theory. These courses are offered at His, *"Heavenly Bird Brain Academy"* run by and for the birds - very similar to most modern universities. God hopes to discover a **Single Theory of God** (STG) algorithm that will forever determine the hierarchical status of all lesser gods. By solving this puzzle he hopes to end wars and establish celestial order, while at the same time provide ample time for sailing and laughing by hearing and telling jokes.

We wish God lots a luck..

The Goddess continues creating new art forms as a way to hopefully modify aberrant animal, including human, spiritual behaviors that throughout history has lead to greedy dumb politics, price gouging, junk bonds, inappropriate language and bad eating habits. On one of her most favorite soft fluffy clouds the Goddess has established a personal meditation foundation called, *"Asps and Apple Trees"* dedicated to the dignity and memory of apple trees and vipers. It is free with ample parking and open daily to the public that can get there.

We wish the Goddess well.

Finally, let us never forget the birds, especially the likes of Falc and Hummy, who continue to add common sense, fresh perspectives, intelligence and humor to our temporal and volatile existence, just as they did at sea for First Time Ark-Boater Noah.

Hummy teaches an *"Advanced Course on Unconventional Flight Theory and Practice"*. Falc offers an entire degree program on, *"How to Win and Lose at Poker and Religion"*. His degree courses are always oversubscribed.

In closing we wish all birds the very best – they deserve it.

On days off from their professorial duties they all; God, Goddess, Noah, Sarah, Falc and Hummy return to the bridge of Captain Noah's ark, wistfully reminiscing about their former arking/sailing days - while of course sipping vintage Askovian rutabaga beer, wondering what comes next and telling jokes. They refer to this looming next big event as God's Big Laugh. No mention is ever made of the Big KaBoom or Big Drown.

I, your faithful Noah messenger Viggo, await further revelations so I can complete the promised expose' titled: *"Inside the CB&G"*. See you all at the Celestial Bar & Grill. Until then – Happy arking/sailing – mates and by all means be happy.

Ho, Ho, ark-ing we must go, Ho, Ho
-Captain Noah

The BIG LAUGH ERA HAS BEGUN

ENJOY SAILING

CAPTAIN NOAH'S
TEN CARDINAL RULES
FOR ALL ARKER/SAILORS

1. Before leaving a slip or mooring make sure you become God's buddy and He yours.

2. Have a strong obedient, but not too obedient, first mate on board, spouses are in general fantastic, but can at times be challenging.

3. Make sure your first mate knows how to cook, clean and entertain - - willingly.

4. Curry the favor of all birds, as they teasingly circle about your boat, they know lots you don't and never will. Talk to them often.

5. Never ever leave port without beer and a basic backup brew kit including essential ingredients.

6. Always have a backup plan for Rule 5.

7. Never look back, it is a dead giveaway that you are paranoid inviting disaster. There is always the chance for another shower.

8. As time permits always keep refreshing your arithmetic skills.

9. Never be in a hurry, rest assured, what you don't do today will still be there to do tomorrow. Relax and laugh!

10. Finally and most importantly. Give God a little slack if weather, crew and seas are less than ideal. He has a lot on his mind and many chores in His topsy-turvy universe to worry about.